J. G. Swift MacNeill

English Interference with Irish Industries

J. G. Swift MacNeill

English Interference with Irish Industries

ISBN/EAN: 9783744726658

Printed in Europe, USA, Canada, Australia, Japan

Cover: Foto ©Suzi / pixelio.de

More available books at **www.hansebooks.com**

ENGLISH INTERFERENCE

WITH

IRISH INDUSTRIES.

BY

J. G. SWIFT MACNEILL, M.A.,

CHRIST CHURCH, OXFORD; BARRISTER-AT-LAW, PROFESSOR OF CONSTITUTIONAL AND CRIMINAL
LAW IN THE HONOURABLE SOCIETY OF THE KING'S INNS, DUBLIN; AND AUTHOR
OF "THE IRISH PARLIAMENT: WHAT IT WAS, AND WHAT IT DID."

———◆◆———

CASSELL & COMPANY, LIMITED:

LONDON, PARIS, NEW YORK & MELBOURNE.

1886.

ENGLISH INTERFERENCE

with

IRISH INDUSTRIES

CASSELL & COMPANY, LIMITED

PREFACE.

AGRICULTURE is at the present time almost the only industry in Ireland. This fact has frequently been noticed and deplored. Public men of widely different views on other matters agree in their estimate of Ireland's economic condition, of which they give but one explanation. Thus Mr. Gladstone, on the introduction of the Irish Land Bill in April, 1881, spoke of "that old and standing evil of Ireland, that land-hunger, which must not be described as if it were merely an infirmity of the people for it, and really means land scarcity."* "In Ireland," says Mr. Bright, "land, from certain causes that are not difficult to discover, is the only thing for the employment of the people, with the exception of some portion of the country in the North; the income for the maintenance of their homes, and whatever comfort they have, or prospect of saving money for themselves or their families, comes from the cultivation of the soil, and scarcely at all from those various resources to which the people of England have recourse in the course of their industrial lives."†

* Hansard, 260, Third Series, p. 893.
† Hansard, 261, Third Series, p. 96.

"It is generally admitted, I think, on both sides of the House," Mr. Bright observes in another debate, "that in discussing the Irish question one fact must always be kept in mind—that is, that apart from the land of Ireland there are few, if any, means of subsistence for the population, and, consequently, there has always been for its possession an exceptional and unnatural demand. This, again, has led to most serious abuses, including nearly all those constant causes of trouble and complaint we are for ever hearing of in Ireland."*

"The truth is," says Mr. Chaplin, from his place in the House of Commons, "that the English Parliament and the English people are mainly responsible for those conditions of the country which have driven the people to the land, and the land alone, for their support. It was not always so; there were other industries in Ireland in former days, which flourished, and flourished to a considerable extent, until they first aroused, and were afterwards suppressed by, the selfish fears and commercial jealousy of England— England, who was alarmed at a rivalry and competition that she dreaded at the hands and from the resources and energy of the Irish people." † "I am convinced that it is in the history of these cruel laws that lies the secret of that fatal competition for the land, in which—and it may well be a just retribution upon us—the source of all the troubles

* Hansard, 261, Third Series, pp. 831, 832.
† Hansard, 261, Third Series, p. 851.

and all the difficulties that you have to deal with will be found."*

"To understand the Irish land question of to-day," writes Sir C. Russell, the present Attorney-General for England, "it is necessary to look back. I have no desire needlessly to rake up bygone wrongs. I wish to Heaven the Irish people could forget the past. For them it is in the main a melancholy retrospect. But England ought not to forget the past—until, at least, a great act of reparation has been done. Even among men of some education in England, remarkable ignorance of the evil wrought in past times by England towards Ireland prevails. There is, indeed, a vague general impression that in very remote times England, when engaged in the endeavour to conquer Ireland, was guilty of cruelties, as most conquering nations are, but that those things have done very little harm ; that their effects have ceased to tell, and that the only purpose served by keeping alive their memory is to irritate the temper of the Irish people and prompt them to look back rather than look forward. Emphatically I say this is not so. The effects have not ceased. It is not too much to say that Ireland and Irishmen of to-day are such as English government has made them." Sir Charles Russell then proceeds to place foremost among "the agencies employed by England which have left enduring evil marks upon

* Hansard, 261, Third Series, p. 853.

Ireland," "the direct legislation avowedly contrived to hinder the development of Irish commerce and manufactures." *

"If people felt impatient with the Irish," said Mr. Fawcett, addressing a political meeting at Shoreditch on November 2nd, 1881, "they should remember that the Irish were, to a great extent, what England had made them. If there were some Irishmen now displaying bitter hostility to England, it should be remembered that for a long time Ireland had been treated as if she had been a hostile or a foreign country. A mass of vexatious restrictions were imposed on her industry, and it was thought that if any branch of Irish trade interfered with English profits, that branch of Irish trade was immediately to be discouraged. For a long time, for instance, to please the agricultural interests of this country, the importation of live cattle from Ireland was absolutely prohibited."

These statements of leading public men are strong evidence of the far-reaching effects upon Ireland of a system which Mr. John Morley, writing on a literary topic, has not hesitated to designate as "the atrocious fiscal policy of Great Britain,"† and for which Earl Cowper, speaking at Belfast as Lord-Lieutenant of Ireland, could find no gentler adjectives than "unjust and iniquitous."‡

* "New Views on Ireland," by C. Russell, Q.C., M.P., pp. 83, 84.
† "English Men of Letters"—"Edmund Burke," by John Morley, p. 76.
‡ *Freeman's Journal,* Nov. 24th, 1881.

In the following pages I propose to exhibit summarily the material injuries inflicted upon Ireland by the commercial or anti-commercial arrangements of Great Britain. With this view, I will endeavour to sketch in outline the political relations of Ireland to Great Britain which rendered such arrangements possible (Chap. I.) ; the principal laws made by the English Parliament in restraint of Irish trade stating them in a plain and popular manner (Chap. II.) ; the opposition of the English Government to the efforts of the Irish Parliament to promote Irish trade (Chap. III.) ; the immediate effects of English legislation on Irish trade (Chap. IV.) ; the Irish Volunteer Movement and free trade (Chap. V.) ; the commercial arrangements between Great Britain and Ireland, 1782–1800 (Chap. VI.); the commercial arrangements effected between Great Britain and Ireland by the Act of Legislative Union (Chap. VII.).

In this inquiry I will, as far as possible, confine myself to an examination of the statutes, which will speak for themselves ; to the journals of the Parliaments of England and Ireland ; and to the statements of contemporary speakers and writers whose accuracy has not, so far as I am aware, been impeached.

CONTENTS.

ENGLISH INTERFERENCE

WITH

IRISH INDUSTRIES.

———◆———

CHAPTER I.

THE POLITICAL RELATIONS OF IRELAND TO GREAT BRITAIN.

THE interference of the English Government with Irish trade before 1782 was twofold, direct and indirect. The direct interference arose from statutes passed in the English Parliament in restraint of Irish commerce. The indirect interference arose from the influence of the English Government over the legislation of the Irish Parliament, under the provisions of the statute known as Poynings' Act.

"From the admitted dependence," says Mr. Butt, " of the Crown of Ireland upon that of England, arose the claim of the English Parliament to legislate for Ireland. Over all the colonies and dependencies of the British Crown, the British Parliament had exercised the right of legislation. Over Ireland they asserted the same right. I need not tell you how fiercely. it was contested, and that it was finally abandoned in 1782. But, up to 1782, the right was asserted, and occasionally exercised." *

These English statutes were chiefly aimed against the Irish manufactures, and were, of course, clear violations of Ireland's Parliamentary independence. The 6th Geo. I. passed by the English Parliament † claimed the power of British legislation over Ireland, a power which had been exercised long previously. "If that power," said Mr. O'Connell, "so claimed, had really existed, where was the necessity for passing that statute ? and while this Act proclaims the slavery of Ireland, it admits the pre-existence of freedom." ‡

The nature and effects of Poynings' Act, and the control given to the English Government by its provisions over Irish legislation, are thus concisely stated by Mr. Butt: "To complete our view of the Irish Parliament, we must remember that by an Act of that Parliament itself a most important restriction was placed upon its legislative powers. By an Irish Act of Parliament, passed in the reign of Henry VII., in the year 1495, it was enacted that no bill should be presented to the Irish Parliament until the heads of it had been submitted to the English Privy Council, and certified as approved of under the Great Seal of England. This law is known as

---

* "Proceedings of the Home Rule Conference," 1873, p. 8.
† 6 Geo. I., c. 5 (Eng.).
‡ " Report of the Discussion in the Dublin Corporation on Repeal of the Union," 1843, p. 23.

Poynings' Law, from the name of the person who was Lord Deputy when it was passed. This law was a matter entirely distinct from any claim of the English Parliament to legislate for Ireland; it was a law of the Irish Parliament itself, passed by the King, Lords, and Commons of Ireland, deriving its authority from a source entirely independent of the English claim, and continuing in force when that claim was abandoned. The original law required the assent of the English Privy Council to be given to the intended bill before Parliament met. In the reign of Queen Mary it was modified so as to admit of that assent being given while Parliament was sitting; but that assent was still necessary to authorise the introduction of the bill. With this modification the law of Poynings continued in force up to 1782." *

We see, accordingly, that England claimed or exercised direct legislative control in her own Parliament over Ireland; while no Irish bills could become law or, indeed, in strictness, be introduced into the Irish Parliament without the sanction of the English Privy Council.†

"Ireland," says Mr. Froude, "was regarded as a colony to be administered, not for her own benefit, but for the convenience of the mother country." ‡

---

* " Proceedings of the Home Rule Conference," 1873, pp. 8, 9.

† For further account of the constitution and powers of the Irish Parliament, see " The Irish Parliament: What it Was, and What it Did," by J. G. Swift MacNeill, published by Cassell & Company, Limited.

‡ " English in Ireland," vol. i., p. 178.

CHAPTER II.

ENGLISH LEGISLATION IN RESTRAINT OF IRISH TRADE.

PERSONS familiar with the relative economic conditions of Great Britain and Ireland at the present
time, will find it difficult to realise that at one period
Ireland enjoyed natural advantages in no respect inferior to those of the sister country.   This, before the
development of steam-power, was undoubtedly the
fact.   This would be still the case were it not for the
dearth of coal in Ireland.*   The evidence of public

---

* Ireland, however, has natural advantages which must not be for-
gotten in any estimate of her economical position, and which, although
they do not compensate her for the want of coal, would under proper
application do much to promote her prosperity.   Thus Mr. O'Connell,
towards the conclusion of his speech in his own defence, in the State
Trials of 1844, says: "The country is intersected with noble
estuaries.   Ships of 500 tons' burthen ride into the heart of the
country, safe from every wind that blows.   No country possesses such
advantages for commerce ; the machinery of the world might be turned
by the water-power of Ireland.   Take the map and dissect it, and you
will find that a good harbour is not more remote from any spot in Ireland than thirty miles." (R. v. O'Connell, p. 649.)   Mr. Chaplin, in the
speech to which I have referred, remarks : "No doubt Ireland does
possess exceptional advantages in water-power which might be turned to
great advantage." (Hansard, 261, Third Series, p. 836.)   Ireland is not,
however, absolutely devoid of coal.   "Though," says Mr. C. Dawson,
"we make no boast of our mineral treasures, they are, according to

men of the last century, who were well acquainted
with the circumstances of both countries, is on this
point conclusive. " Ireland," writes Edmund Burke
in 1778, " is a country in the same climate and of the
same natural qualities and productions with this
(England)."* " In Ireland," writes Hely Hutchinson
in 1779, "the climate, soil, growth, and productions
are the same as in England."† Plunket, in his speech
against the Union, delivered in the Irish Parliament
on the 15th of January, 1800, draws a comparison
between England and Ireland, in which he describes
England as "another happy little island placed beside
her (Ireland) in the bosom of the Atlantic, of little
more than double her territory and population, and
possessing resources not nearly so superior to her

competent authority, well worthy of development. According to Professor Hull, the Leinster coal-basin contains 118 million tons, only out-
putting 83,000 tons per annum. In the North, especially in Tyrone,
at Coal Island, there are 17,000 acres of coal-bed (30,000,000 tons),
which the Professor says are by far the most valuable in Ireland. In
the other districts in Ireland there are over 70,000,000 tons. Sir R.
Kane supports the suggestion that borings should be made by the
Government in this district to ascertain if the mineral wealth existed to
the extent computed by Professor Hull, and he adds that when the
panic arose in England about the duration of its coal supply, coal was
looked for then outside the limits of the recognised coal-fields, and
following them down into the Chalk in Kent and other places, of which
Ireland was one." (" The Influence of an Irish Parliament on Irish
Industries," Lecture by Mr. Charles Dawson, *Freeman's Journal*,
Jan. 5, 1886.)

* " Burke on Irish Affairs," by M. Arnold, p. 101.

† " Commercial Restraints," p. 156. Mr. Secretary Orde, in introducing in the Irish House of Commons, in 1785, the Commercial
Propositions, said : " Great Britain was aware of the preferable commercial situation of Ireland." (" Irish Debates," iv., p. 120.)

B

wants."* Mr. Froude's researches lead him to a similar conclusion : "Before the days of coal and steam, the unlimited water-power of Ireland gave her natural advantages in the race of manufactures, which, if she had received fair play, would have attracted thither thousands of skilled immigrants."†

I do not propose to furnish an exhaustive statement of the various laws passed by the English Parliament for the avowed purpose of destroying Irish trade and manufactures. I will deal only with the salient features of that system whose effects are, at the present day, sadly apparent.

Till the reign of Charles II., England placed no restriction on Irish commerce or manufactures. "Before the' Restoration," says Lord North, in the British House of Commons, "they (the Irish) enjoyed every commercial advantage and benefit in common with England." ‡ "Ireland," writes Hely Hutchinson, "was in possession of the English common law and of Magna Charta. The former secures the subject in the enjoyment of property of every kind, and by the latter *the liberties of all the ports of the Kingdom are established.*" § "Our trade," says Mr. Gardiner in the Irish House of Commons, "was guaranteed by Magna Charta, our exports acknowledged by that venerable statute—no treaty was made in which we

* "Life and Speeches of Lord Plunket," by the Right Hon. D. Plunket, vol. i., pp. 173, 174.
† "English in Ireland," vol. i., p. 178.
‡ "Parliamentary Debates," xv., p. 175.
§ "Commercial Restraints," p. 164.

were not nominally or virtually included." * By one
of the provisions of Poynings' Law, passed in 1495, all
statutes hitherto in force in England were extended to
Ireland. Before that enactment, however, Ireland is
expressly mentioned in several English commercial
statutes, in which clauses are inserted for the protection of her trade.† "At this period (1495)," says Hely
Hutchinson, "the English commercial system and the
Irish, so far as it depended on English statute law,
was the same; and before this period, so far as it
depended on the common law and Magna Charta,
was also the same. From that time till the 15th of
King Charles II., which takes in a period of 167 years,
the commercial constitution of Ireland was as much
favoured and protected as that of England." ‡

The first Navigation Act of 1660 put England and
Ireland on exact terms of equality.§ This community
of rights was emphasised by an Act of the following
year, which provided that foreign-built ships should
not have the privilege of ships belonging to England

* "Irish Debates," iii., p. 123. Henry, Archbishop of Dublin, is
mentioned in Magna Charta as one of the barons whose "advice" led
to the signing of that instrument by John. This prelate, Henry de
Loundres, or "the Londoner," erected St. Patrick's Church, Dublin,
into a cathedral, and created the offices of Precentor, Chancellor,
Treasurer, and Dean—the last a post destined to be rendered famous
five centuries later by the incumbency of Swift. Strange that at far-
distant periods of time St. Patrick's Cathedral should be associated
with the names of two illustrious assertors of liberty !

† These enactments are mentioned in the "Commercial Restraints,"
pp. 164—169.

‡ "Commercial Restraints," p. 169.

§ 12 Car. II., c. 18.

B 2

and Ireland.* " But," as Mr. Froude observes, " the
equality of privilege lasted only till the conclusion of
the settlement and till the revenue had been assigned
to the Crown." †   In the amended Navigation Act of
1663, Ireland was left out. Lord North, on December 13,
1779, when Prime Minister of England, in introducing a
bill to abrogate some of the restrictions on Irish trade,
thus described the Act of 1663 : " The first commercial restriction was laid on Ireland not directly, but by
a side-wind and by deductive interpretation. When
the Act (the Navigation Act of 1660) first passed
there was a general governing clause for giving bonds
to perform the conditions of the Act ; but when the
Act was amended in the 15 Car. II. the word ' Ireland
was omitted, whence a conclusion was drawn that the
Acts of the two preceding Parliaments, 12 & 13
and 14 Car. II., were thereby repealed, though it was
as clearly expressed in those Acts as it was possible
for words to convey, that ships built in Ireland,
navigated with the people thereof, were deemed
British, and qualified to trade to and from British
Plantations, and that ships built in Ireland and
navigated with his Majesty's subjects of Ireland, were
entitled to the same abatement and privileges to which
imports and exports of goods in British-made ships were
entitled by the book of rates. Ireland was, however,
omitted in the manner he had already mentioned."‡

* 13 & 14 Car. II., c. 11, s. 6.
† " English in Ireland," i., p. 179.
‡ " Parliamentary Debates," xv., pp. 175, 176. Edmund Burke,
speaking in the British House of Commons, on May 6th, 1778, thus

This Act, which is entitled "An Act for the Encouragement of Trade," prohibited all *exports* from Ireland to the colonies.* It likewise prohibited the importation of Irish cattle into England. It states that "a very great part of the richest and best land of this kingdom (England) is, and cannot so well otherwise be employed and made use of as in the feeding and fattening of cattle, and that by the coming in of late in vast numbers of cattle already fatted such lands are in many places much fallen, and like daily to fall more in their rents and values, and in consequence other lands also, to the great prejudice, detriment, and impoverishment of this kingdom;"† and it imposes a penalty on every head of great cattle imported. A subsequent British Act declares the importation of Irish cattle into England to be "a publick and common nuisance." ‡ It likewise forbids the importation of beef, pork, or bacon. Butter and cheese from Ireland were subsequently excluded, and the previous statute excluding cattle was made perpetual.§ In 1670 the

commented on this transaction : "In the 12 Car. II. the Navigation Acts passed, extending to Ireland, as well as England. A kind of left-handed policy, however, had deprived her of the freedom she enjoyed under that Act, and she had ever since remained under the most cruel, oppressive, and unnatural restrictions." ("Parliamentary Debates," viii., p. 265.)

* Except victuals, servants, horses, and salt, for the fisheries of New England and Newfoundland.

† 15 Car. II., c. 7, s. 13.

‡ 18 Car. II., c. 2.

§ 32 Car. II., c. 2. Irish cattle were readmitted into England by the 32 Geo. II., c. 11. This was but a temporary enactment, but

exportation to Ireland from the English Plantations
of sugar, tobacco, cotton-wool, indigo, ginger, fustic
or other dyeing wood, the growth of the said Plantations, was prohibited by statute. It is stated in
the statute that this restraint was intended by the
Act of 1663, but not effectively expressed.*

"There are," says Lord North, "anecdotes still
extant relative to the real causes of those harsh and
restrictive laws. They were supposed to have
originated in a dislike or jealousy of the growing
power of the then Duke of Ormonde, who, from his
great estate and possessions in Ireland, was supposed to have a personal interest in the prosperity of that kingdom. Indeed, so far was this
spirit carried, whether from personal enmity to the
Duke of Ormonde, from narrow prejudices, or
a blind policy, that the Parliament of England
passed a law to prohibit the importation of Irish
lean cattle." †

An extensive and profitable cattle trade which
Ireland had established with Bristol, Milford, and
Liverpool was annihilated by this legislation. With
the restriction of her chief exports, her shipping trade
suffered a simultaneous eclipse. Such direct trade as
she retained was with France, Spain, and Portugal, as
if England wished to force her, in spite of herself, to

---

it was renewed without difficulty.   Hely Hutchinson says it was
acknowledged that the importation did not lower English rents.
"Commercial Restraints," p. 86.)

   * 22 & 23 Car. II., c. 26.
   † "Parliamentary Debates," xv., p. 176.

feel the Catholic countries to be her best friends.* Till 1663 the Irish had, according to Carte, no commerce but with England, and scarcely entertained a thought of trafficking with other countries.† This writer gives melancholy evidence as to the immediate effect of that restrictive legislation. " The people," he says, "had no money to pay the subsidies granted by Parliament, and their cattle was grown such a drug, that horses that used to be sold for 30s. were now sold for dogs' meat at 12d. apiece, and beeves that brought before 50s. were now sold for ten." ‡

Deprived of their trade, the Irish people, under the guidance of the Duke of Ormonde, set themselves resolutely to improve their own manufactures. " The history of Ireland," says Chief Justice Whiteside, " for nigh half a century may be read in the life, actions, and adventures of this able, virtuous, and illustrious man. His chivalrous courage, his unflinching loyalty, his disinterested patriotism, mark him out as one of the foremost men of his noble family, and as one of the finest characters of his age." § In 1692, Lord Sydney, the Lord-Lieutenant, in his speech from the Throne, was able, from his former knowledge of the country, to testify to its vastly increased prosperity.‖ " The cause of this prosperity should," says Hely Hutchinson

* " English in Ireland," i. 180.
† Carte's " Ormonde," ii. 357.
‡ Carte's " Ormonde," ii. 329.
§ " Life and Death of the Irish Parliament," p. 69.
‖ " Irish Commons' Journals," ii. 577.

" be mentioned.   James, the first Duke of Ormonde,
whose memory should ever be revered by every friend
of Ireland, to heal the wound that this country had
received by the prohibition of the export of her cattle
to England, obtained from Charles II. a letter, dated
the 23rd of March, 1667, by which he directed that
all restraints upon the exportation of commodities of
the growth or manufacture of Ireland to foreign parts
should be taken off, but not to interfere with the
Plantation laws, or the charters to the trading com-
panies, and that this should be notified to his subjects
of this kingdom, which was accordingly done by a
proclamation from the Lord-Lieutenant and Council ;
and at the same time, by his Majesty's permission,
they prohibited the importation from Scotland of
linen, woollen, and other manufactures and commodities, as drawing large sums of money out of Ireland,
and a great hindrance to manufactures.   His grace
successfully executed his schemes of national improvement, having by his own constant attention, the
exertion of his extensive influence, and the most
princely munificence, greatly advanced the woollen
and revived the linen manufactures."* Ormonde
established a woollen manufactory at Clonmel, " the
capital of his county palatine of Tipperary, bringing
over five hundred Walloon families from the neigh-
bourhood of Canterbury to carry it on, and giving
houses and land on long leases with only an acknow-
ledgment instead of rent from the undertakers.   Also

* " Commercial Restraints," p. 20.

in Kilkenny and Carrick-on-Suir the duke established large colonies of those industrious foreigners, so well skilled in the preparation and weaving of wool."*

The woollen manufacture was the "true and natural staple of the Irish, their climate and extensive sheep-grounds insuring to them a steady and cheap supply of the raw material, much beyond their home consumption."† It was cultivated for several years after the Revolution without any interference by the English Parliament. It had, however, long previously excited the jealous hatred of English statesmen. " I am of opinion,"says Lord Strafford,writing,when Lord-Lieutenant, from Ireland to Charles I. in 1634, " that all wisdom advises to keep this kingdom as much subordinate and dependent upon England as is possible, and holding them from the manufacture of wool (which, unless otherwise directed, I shall by all means discourage), and then enforcing them to fetch their clothing from thence, and to take their salt from the King (being that which preserves and gives value to all their native staple commodities), how can they depart from us without nakedness and beggary ? Which is of itself so mighty a consideration that a small profit should not bear it down." ‡ This proposal I

* " Irish Wool and Woollens," by S. A., p. 67.
† "Report from the Select Committee on the Linen Trade of Ireland, 6th June, 1825."
‡ " Life of Thomas Wentworth, Earl of Strafford," by Elizabeth Cooper, i., pp. 185, 186. Miss Cooper comments severely "on the stolid unconsciousness of wrongdoing by such a design, the undreamed-

will not characterise. " In 1673, Sir William Temple, at the request of the Earl of Essex, then Viceroy of Ireland, publicly proposed that the manufacture of woollens (except in the inferior branches) should be relinquished in Ireland as tending to interfere prejudicially with the English trade. In all probability

of suspicion that such a proposal could be received with any other feeling than that of approbation." It is but just to the memory of Strafford to state that he endeavoured to develop the linen manufacture in Ireland. He sent to Holland for flax seed, and invited Flemish and French artisans to settle in Ireland. " In order to stimulate the new industry, the earl himself embarked in it, and expended not less than £30,000 of his private fortune in the enterprise. It was afterwards made one of the grounds of his impeachment that he had obstructed the industry of the country by introducing new and unknown processes into the manufacture of flax. It was, nevertheless, greatly to the credit of the.earl that he should have endeavoured to improve the industry of Ireland by introducing the superior processes employed by foreign artisans, and had he not attempted to turn the improved flax manufacture to his own advantage by. erecting it into a personal monopoly, he might have been entitled to regard as a genuine benefactor of Ireland." (Smiles's " Huguenots," p. 126.) Dr. Smiles, in this passage, speaks of the linen manufacture as a "new industry." The " Report from the Select Committee on the Linen Trade of Ireland " states that that trade was " first planted in Ireland by Lord Strafford " (Appendix, p. 6), and Miss Cooper gives him credit " for the establishment of the linen manufacture in Ireland." (" Life of Lord Strafford," i., p. 346.) These statements are not, I think, historically correct. Mr. Lecky shows that, although Lord Strafford stimulated the linen trade, he did not found it. " The linen manufacture may, indeed, be dimly traced far back into Irish history. It is noticed in an English poem in the early part of the fifteenth century. A century later Guicciardini, in his ' Description of the Low Countries,' mentions coarse linen as among the products imported from Ireland to Antwerp. Strafford had done much to encourage it, and after the calamities of the Cromwellian period the Duke of Ormonde had laboured with some success to revive it." (" England in the Eighteenth Century," ii., pp. 211, 212.) See also, for some very valuable remarks on this subject, " Irish Wool and Woollens," pp. 63, 64.

the Irish manufacturers of broadcloths would gain on their English rivals, and the improvement of woollen fabrics in Ireland, argued the statesman, 'would give so great a damp to the trade of England, that it seems not fit to be encouraged here.' "*   These suggestions were not immediately acted on.   In 1660 no doubt the exportation of Irish woollen goods to England was prohibited, but this enactment did not at the time inflict material injury on Ireland.†

In 1697 a bill was introduced into the English House of Commons, forbidding all export from Ireland of her woollen manufactures.   It reached the House of Lords, but Parliament was dissolved before it passed its final stage in that assembly.

The destruction of the woollen trade is one of the most disastrous chapters of Irish history.   The circumstances attending this transaction are detailed in an Appendix to the "Report from the Select Committee on the Linen Trade of Ireland," which was printed on the 6th of June, 1825, by order of the House of Commons.   This paper was prepared by Lord Oriel, who, as Mr. Foster, was Chancellor of the Irish Exchequer and afterwards Speaker of the Irish House of Commons.   He was one of the greatest authorities of his time on trade and finance.   The Report thus describes an incident which is, I believe, without parallel.

* "Irish Wool and Woollens," p. 70.   See also Newenham on "The Population of Ireland," pp. 40, 41.

† 12 Car. II., c. 4.   A duty equal to a prohibition was laid on those goods.

" This export (the woollen) was supposed to inter-
ere, and very probably did, with the export from
Britain, and a plan was in consequence undertaken
there to annihilate the woollen trade of Ireland, and
to confine us to the linen manufacture in its place.

"Accordingly an Act was passed in England,
1696 (7 & 8 Will., c. 39), for inviting foreign Protestants to settle in Ireland, as the preamble recites,
and with that view enacting that the imports of all
sorts of hemp and flax, and all the productions thereof, should from thenceforth be admitted duty free
from Ireland into England, giving a preference by
that exemption from duty to the linen manufacture
of Ireland over the foreign, estimated at the time, as
a report of the Irish House of Commons, on the 11th
February, 1774, states, to be equal to 25 per cent.

" This happened in 1696, and in pursuance of the
foregoing plan both Houses of the English Parliament addressed King William ón the 9th June, 1698.

" The Lords stated in their Address that ' the growing manufacture of cloth in Ireland, both by the
cheapness of all sorts of necessaries of life, and the
goodness of materials for making all manner of cloth,
doth invite your subjects of England, with their families and servants, to leave their habitations and settle
there, to the increase of the woollen manufacture in
Ireland, which makes your loyal subjects in this kingdom very apprehensive that the further growth of it
may greatly prejudice the said manufacture here,
by which the trade of this nation and the value of

lands will greatly decrease, and the number of your people be much lessened here; wherefore we humbly beseech your most Sacred Majesty that your Majesty would be pleased, in the most public and effectual way that may be, to declare to all your subjects of Ireland that the growth and increase of the woollen manufacture there hath long and will be ever looked upon with great jealousy by all your subjects of this kingdom, and if not timely remedied, may occasion very strict laws totally to prohibit and suppress the same; and, on the other hand, if they turn their industry to the settling and improving the *linen manufacture*, for which generally the lands are very proper, *they shall receive all the countenance, favour, and protection from your royal influence for the encouragement and promotion of the linen manufacture to all the advantage and profit they can be capable of.'*

"The Commons stated their sentiments at the same time in the following terms: 'We,* your Majesty's most dutiful and loyal subjects, the Commons in Parliament assembled, being very sensible that the wealth and power of this kingdom do in a great measure depend on the preservation of the woollen manufacture as much as possible entire to this realm, think it becomes us, like our ancestors, to be jealous of the increase and establishment of it elsewhere, and to use our utmost endeavours to prevent it. And, therefore, we cannot without trouble observe that Ireland, which is dependent on and protected

* " English Commons' Journals," xii., p. 338.

by England in the enjoyment of all they have, and which is so proper for the linen manufacture, the establishment and growth of which there would be so enriching to themselves, and so profitable to England, should of late apply itself to the woollen manufacture, to the great prejudice of the trade of this kingdom, and so unwillingly promote the linen trade, which would benefit both themselves and us ; the consequence whereof will necessitate your Parliament of England to interpose to prevent the mischief that threatens us, unless your Majesty by your authority and great wisdom shall find means to secure the trade of England, by making your subjects of Ireland to pursue the joint interests of both kingdoms. And we do most humbly implore your Majesty's protection and favour in this matter, that you will make it your royal care, and enjoin all those you employ in Ireland to make it their care, and use their utmost diligence, to hinder the exportation of wool from Ireland except to be imported hither, and for discouraging the woollen manufacture and encouraging the linen manufacture of Ireland, *to which we shall always be ready to give our utmost assistance.'*

"His Majesty thus replied to the Commons* :—'*I shall do all that in me lies to* discourage the woollen manufacture in Ireland *and encourage the linen manufacture there,* and to promote the trade of England.'

"Stronger declarations could not well be made

* "English Commons' Journals," xii. 339.

than in these Addresses and answers, that if the Irish
would come into the compact of giving up their then
great staple of woollens to England, and cultivating
the linens in lieu thereof, they should receive '*all the
countenance, favour, and protection for the encouragement and promotion of their linen manufacture to all
the advantages their kingdom was capable of,*' that
the Commons would always be ready to give their
utmost assistance, and his Majesty would do all that
in him lay *to encourage the linen manufacture there;*
and they had the effect of inducing the Parliament of
Ireland to accede, as will appear from what follows.

"The Lords Justices of Ireland say, in their speech
to the Irish Parliament, the 27th September, 1698:*
'Amongst those bills there is one for the encouragement of the linen and hempen manufactures. At our
first meeting we recommended to you that matter,
and we have now endeavoured to render that bill
practicable and useful for that effect, and as such we
now recommend it to you. The settlement of this
manufacture will contribute much to people the
country, and will be found much more advantageous
to this kingdom than the woollen manufacture, which,
being the settled staple trade of England, can never
be encouraged here for that purpose; *whereas the
linen and hempen manufactures will not only be encouraged, as consistent with the trade of England, but
will render the trade of this kingdom both useful and
necessary to England.*'

* "Irish Commons' Journals," ii., p. 241.

"‗The Commons replied : ' We pray leave to assure your Excellencies that we shall heartily endeavour to establish a linen and hempen manufacture here, and to render the same useful to England, as well as advantageous to this kingdom; and we hope to find such a *temperament* in respect to the woollen trade here that the same may not be injurious to England.'*
In pursuance of this answer they evinced that *temperament* most effectually by passing an Act † for laying prohibitory duties on the export of *their own* woollen manufacture—thus accepting the national compact and fully performing their part of the agreement, and by that performance giving an incontrovertible claim to Ireland upon England, and consequently upon Great Britain, for a perpetual encouragement of the linen manufacture ' *to all the advantage and profit that Ireland should at any time be capable of.*'

" It is to be observed that so anxious was England to confirm and enforce this ratification given by Ireland, that their Parliament soon after passed a law affecting to enact what subsequent times have shown it was incompetent to, and which we therefore here mention merely to point out the stress which England laid on the sacrifice made by Ireland of its great and natural staple trade, in exchange for a new staple resting on a material not the natural growth of the country, and the establishment of which was but in its infancy, though nurtured for near sixty years by the Government of the kingdom. The Act we refer to is the 10 & 11 Will. III., cap. 10, which recites 'that wool and the woollen manufacture of cloth, serge, bays, kerseys, and other stuffs made or mixed with wool, are the greatest and most profitable commodities of the kingdom, on which the value of lands and the trade of the nation do chiefly depend; that great quantities of the *like manufactures* have of late been made, and *are daily increasing in the kingdom of Ireland*, and in the English Plantations in America, *and are exported from thence to foreign markets heretofore supplied from England :* all which inevitably tends to injure the value of lands, and to ruin the trade and woollen manufactures of the realm ; and that for the prevention thereof the export of wool and of the woollen manufacture from Ireland be prohibited under the forfeiture of goods and ship, and a penalty of £500 for every such offence.'"

Ireland's woollen manufacture was thus sacrificed to England's commercial jealousy.* I will give hereafter some account of the widespread misery this industrial calamity entailed. It might have been

---

* Subsequent Acts completed this annihilation. "The next Act," says Lord North, after enumerating the Acts mentioned above, "was an Act of the 5th Geo. I., the next the 5th and 12th of the late King (Geo. II.), which last went so far as to prohibit the export of a kind of woollen manufacture called waddings, and one or two other articles excepted out of the 10th and 11th of King William ; but these three last Acts swept everything before them." (" Parliamentary Debates," xv. 176, 177.)

C

expected that the solemn compact for the encouragement of the linen trade would have been scrupulously observed. This, however, was not the case. The English Parliament deliberately broke faith with the Irish people. This charge I will substantiate by quotations from the speeches of public men in the English Parliament, the words of the English statute book, and the admissions of English writers.

Lord Rockingham, speaking in the English House of Lords on the 11th of May, 1779, "reminded their lordships of the compact made between both kingdoms in King William's time, when the Parliament of Ireland consented to prohibit the export of their own woollen manufacture, in order to give that of England a preference, by laying a duty equal to a full prohibition on every species of woollens, or even of the raw commodity, and of the solemn assurances given by both Houses of the British Parliament that they would give every possible encouragement, and abstain from every measure which could prevent the linen manufacture to be rendered the staple of Ireland. But how had England kept its word? By laying duties or granting bounties to the linens of British manufacture equal to a prohibition of the Irish, and at the same time giving every kind of private and public encouragement to render Scotland a real rival to Ireland in almost every species of her linen fabrics."*

" Ireland," says Lord North when Prime Minister

* " Parliamentary Debates,' vol. xiii., 33ว.

of England, in the speech from which I have previously quoted, " gave up her woollen trade by compact. The compact was an exclusive linen trade,
rather a fair competition with England. Ireland, of
her own accord, gave up the woollen trade by an Act
of her own Legislature, which, when it expired, was
made perpetual by an Act of the British Parliament.
But this compact was no sooner made than it
was violated by England, for, instead of prohibit-
ing foreign linens, duties were laid on and necessarily
collected, so far from amounting to a prohibition on
the import of the Dutch, German, and East Country
linen manufactures, that those manufactures have
been able, after having the duties imposed on them
by the British Parliament, to meet, and in some
instances to undersell, Ireland both in Great Britain
and the West Indies, and several other parts of the
British Empire."*

Writing in 1778 to the opponents of some trifling
relaxation of the commercial restraints of Ireland,
Edmund Burke asks : " Do they forget that the whole
woollen manufacture of Ireland, the most extensive and
profitable of any, and the natural staple of that kingdom, has been in a manner so destroyed by restrictive
laws of *their own*, that in a few years it is probable
they (the Irish) will not be able to wear a coat of their
own fabric ? Is this equality ? Do gentlemen forget
that the understood faith upon which they were persuaded to such an unnatural act has not been kept,

* " Parliamentary Debates," vol. xv., 181.

C 2

and that a linen manufacture has been set up and
highly encouraged against them ? " *

In the year 1750 heavy taxes were laid on the
import to England of sail-cloth made of Irish hemp,
contrary, of course, to the express stipulation of 1698.
An address presented in 1774 to Lord Harcourt, the
Viceroy, by the Irish House of Commons thus describes the effect of this measure : " They had been
confined by law to the manufacture of flax and
hemp. They had submitted to their condition,
and had manufactured these articles to such good
purpose that at one time they had supplied sails for
the whole British navy. Their English rivals had
now crippled them by laying a disabling duty on
their sail-cloths, in the hope of taking the trade out of
their hands, but they had injured Ireland without
benefiting themselves. The British market was now
supplied from Holland and Germany and Russia,
while to the Empire the result was only the ruin of
Ulster and the flight of the Protestant population to
America."†

---

* "Irish Affairs," pp. 112, 113.

† "English in Ireland," vol. ii., p. 177. Mr. Lecky thus suc-
cinctly states the particulars attending the breach of the Linen
Compact :—" The main industry of Ireland had been deliberately
destroyed because it had so prospered that English manufacturers
had begun to regard it as a competitor with their own. It is true,
indeed, that a promise was made that the linen and hempen manufacture should be encouraged as a compensation, but even if it had
been a just principle that a nation should be restricted by force of
law to one or two forms of industry, there was no proportion between
that which was destroyed and that which was to be favoured, and no real
reciprocity established between the two countries." Mr. Lecky having

I have dwelt thus at length on the chief commercial restraints laid on Ireland by the direct legislation of England. This interference was, however, carried to almost every branch of Irish trade. To take a few examples. Lord North in the English Parliament gives the following account of England's dealings with the Irish glass trade :—

"Previous to the 19th Geo. II., Ireland imported glass from other countries, and at length began to make some slow progress in the lower branches of the manufacture itself. By the Act alluded to, however, the Irish were prohibited from importing any kind of glass other than the manufacture of Great

---

stated the antiquity of the linen manufacture and its vicissitudes in Ireland, and having mentioned that " in 1700 the value of the export of Irish linen amounted to little more than £14,000," thus proceeds :— "The English utterly suppressed the existing woollen manufacture in Ireland in order to reserve that industry entirely to themselves, but the English and Scotch continued, as usual, their manufacture of linen. The Irish trade was ruined in 1699, but no legislative encouragement was given to the Irish linen manufacture till 1705, when, at the urgent petition of the Irish Parliament, the Irish were allowed to export their white and brown linens, but these only to the British colonies, and they were not permitted to bring any colonial goods in return. The Irish linen manufacture was undoubtedly encouraged by bounties, but not until 1743, when the country had sunk into a condition of appalling wretchedness. In spite of the compact of 1698, the hempen manufacture was so discouraged that it positively ceased. Disabling duties were imposed on Irish sail-cloth imported into England. Irish checked, striped, and dyed linens were absolutely excluded from the colonies. They were virtually excluded from England by the imposition of a duty of 30 per cent., and Ireland was not allowed to participate in the bounties granted for the exportation of these descriptions of linen from Great Britain to foreign countries."—" Eighteenth Century," vol. ii., pp. 211—212. See also, " An Argument for Ireland," by J. O'Connell, M.P., pp. 147—154.

Britain, and in section 24 of that Act a most extraordinary clause was inserted. It not only ordained
that no glass, the manufacture of that kingdom, should
be exported, but it was penned so curiously, and with
so much severe precision, that no glass of the manufacture of Ireland was to be exported, or so much as
to be laden on any horse or carriage with intent to be
so exported. This was, in his opinion, a very extraordinary stretch of the legislative power of Great
Britain, considering the smallness of the object. The
Act was much, very much complained of in Ireland,
and apparently with very great justice both as to
principle and effect. It was an article of general use
in Ireland. The manufacturers of glass there, when
thus restrained both as to export and import, could
not pretend to vie with the British; the consequence
of which was that the latter, having the whole trade
to themselves, fixed the price of the commodity as
they liked."* By the 9 Anne, c. 12, and 5 Geo. II.,
c. 2, and 7 Geo. II., c. 19, no hops but of British
growth could be imported into Ireland. By the
6 Geo. I., it was enacted that the duty on hops exported from England should not be drawn back in
favour of Irish consumers.†

Irish cotton manufactures imported to England
were subject to an import duty of twenty-five per
cent., while a statute of Geo. I. enacted penalties on

---

* "Parliamentary Debates," vol. xv., 179, 180.
† "Commercial Restraints," pp. 229, 230.

the wearing of such manufactures in Great Britain
unless they were made there.

The raw material for silk came to Ireland through
England. The original import duty in England was
12d. in the pound, of which 3d. in the pound was retained there.*

Irish beer and malt, too, were excluded from
England, whereas English beer and malt were imported into Ireland at a nominal duty. " Hats, gun-
powder, coals, bar-iron, iron-ware, and several other
matters, some of which Ireland had not to export,
and others of which she had very little, were at different times the objects of English restrictions, whenever it was fancied that English interests were at all
threatened by them."†

It was this legislation that caused Edmund Burke
to ask, " Is Ireland united to the Crown of Great
Britain for no other purpose than that we should
counteract the bounty of Providence in her favour,
and in proportion as that bounty has been liberal
that we are to regard it as an evil which is to be
met with in every sort of corrective ? "‡

" England," says Mr. Froude, "governed Ireland
for what she deemed her own interest, making her
calculation on the gross balance of her trade ledgers,
and leaving her moral obligations to accumulate, as if

---

* See " An Argument for Ireland," p. 161.
† " An Argument for Ireland," by J. O'Connell, M.P., p. 161.
‡ Burke on " Irish Affairs," p. 101.

right and wrong had been blotted out of the statute book of the universe." *

"One by one of each of our nascent industries," observes Lord Dufferin, "was either strangled in its birth, or handed over gagged and bound to the jealous custody of the rival interest of England, until at last every fountain of wealth was hermetically sealed, and even the traditions of commercial enterprise have perished through desuetude."

This sketch of English legislation for Irish trade would leave the impression that the Parliaments of Great Britain were as lavish in their efforts to suppress industrial enterprise in that country as any British trader could reasonably desire. It will surprise us to find that this atrocious code was not regarded as sufficiently thorough.

"In the year 1698," says Hely Hutchinson, "two petitions were preferred from Folkestone and Aldborough, stating a singular grievance that they suffered from Ireland 'by the Irish catching herrings at *Waterford and Wexford,* and sending them to the Streights, and thereby *forestalling* and ruining petitioners' markets ;' but these petitioners had the *hard lot* of having motions in their favour rejected."†

---

* "English in Ireland," vol. i., p. 657.

† "Commercial Restraints," pp. 125, 126. See "English Commons' Journals," 22, p. 178. In this summary of the laws enacted by the English Parliament in restraint of Irish trade, I have dealt merely with legislation of a permanent character. "When," says Hely Hutchinson, in 1779, "the commercial restraints of Ireland are the subject, a source of occasional and ruinous restrictions ought not to

be passed over. Since the year 1740 there have been twenty-four embargoes in Ireland, one of which lasted three years." "Commercial Restraints," pp. 231, 232. The system of embargoes called forth the indignation of Arthur Young, the celebrated English traveller. The prohibition of woollens, etc., was, he says, at least advantageous to similar manufactures in England, but "in respect to embargoes, even this shallow pretence is wanting; a whole kingdom is sacrificed and plundered, not to enrich England, but three or four London contractors." See also Lecky's "Eighteenth Century," iv., p. 442.

CHAPTER III.

ENGLISH OPPOSITION TO EFFORTS OF THE IRISH PARLIAMENT IN FAVOUR OF IRISH TRADE.

MR. FOX, speaking in the British House of Commons on the 17th of May, 1782, as a responsible Minister of the Crown, thus stated the nature and effect of the legislation of the English Parliament with reference to Irish trade: "The power of external legislation had been employed against Ireland as an instrument of oppression, to establish an impolitic monopoly in trade, to enrich one country at the expense of the other."* The English Government was, previously to the Revolution of 1782, able to dominate the legislation of the Irish Parliament under the provisions of Poynings' Law. That power was used to induce the Irish Parliament to pass laws prejudicial to the liberties or the commerce of their country, and to prevent the enactment of laws for the protection of Irish liberty, and the development of Irish industrial energies. Thus, when the English Houses of Parliament addressed William III. on the subject of the Irish woollen trade, both Lords and Commons suggested that the King should use his influence to induce the Irish Parliament to restrain that manu-

* " Parliamentary Register," p. 7.

facture, without rendering English legislation for the purpose necessary. A few days after these Addresses were presented, the King wrote to Lord Galway, one of the Lords Justices of Ireland, as follows:—

"The chief thing that must be prevented is that the Irish Parliament take no notice of this here, and that you make effectual laws for the linen manufacture, and discourage as far as possible the woollen. It never was of such importance to have a good session of Parliament."*

Ireland was thus, in the words of Mr. Froude, "invited to apply the knife to her own throat."† "The Irish Houses, in dread of abolition if they refused, relying on the promise of encouragement to their linen trade, and otherwise unable to help themselves, acquiesced." ‡ The enactment which they passed was temporary. Hely Hutchinson says that this law has every appearance of being framed on the part of the Administration. The servile body who assented to it soon had reason to know that to tolerate slavery is to embrace it. The law did not satisfy the English Parliament, who passed the perpetual enactment to which reference has been previously made.§ This is, however, one of the few instances in which the Irish Parliament was prevailed on to pass laws in restraint

* Rapin, xvii., p. 417. The date of this letter is 16th of July, 1698. The matter was so urgent that William III. wrote two letters. See "English in Ireland," i. 297.

† "English in Ireland," vol. i., p. 297.

‡ *Ibid.*, p. 297.

§ 10 & 11 Will. III., c. 10.

of their own trade.   Even in this case the destruction
of the woollen industry was not considered complete
until English legislation gave it a final blow.

The direct attacks on Irish trade were almost
exclusively the work of the English Parliament ;
while the English Privy Council strangled at its birth
every beneficial enactment of the Irish Parliament.

The following instances will explain and illustrate
the difficulties with which the Irish Parliament had to
contend in every effort to promote the material prosperity of their country :—

"With," says Mr. Froude, "their shipping destroyed
by the Navigation Act, their woollen manufactures
taken from them, their trade in all its branches
crippled and confined, the single resource left to those
of the Irish who still nourished dreams of improving
their unfortunate country was agriculture.   The soil
was at least their own, which needed only to be
drained, cleared of weeds, and manured to produce
grass crops and corn crops as rich as the best in
England.   Here was employment for a population
three times more numerous than as yet existed.
Here was a prospect, if not of commercial wealth, yet
of substantial comfort and material abundance." *

After some further observations, Mr. Froude thus
proceeds :—" The tenants were forbidden in their
leases to break or plough the soil.   The people no
longer employed were driven away into holes and
corners, and eked out a wretched subsistence by potato

* "English in Ireland," vol. i., p. 439.

gardens or by keeping starving cattle of their own on the neglected bogs. Their numbers increased, for they married early, and they were no longer liable, as in the old times, to be killed off like dogs in forays. They grew up in compulsory idleness, encouraged once more in their inherited dislike of labour,* and inured to wretchedness and hunger; and on every failure of the potato crop, hundreds of thousands were starving. Of corn very little was grown anywhere in Ireland. It was imported from England, Holland, Italy, and France, but in quantities unequal to any sudden demand. The disgrace of allowing a nation of human beings to subsist upon such conditions forced itself at last on the conscience of the Irish Parliament, and though composed of landowners who were

---

* The charge of indolence which Mr. Froude has here preferred against the Irish peasantry has frequently been refuted. The accusation is an old one. Speaking in the Irish House of Commons in 1784, the Right Hon. Luke Gardiner thus repelled it :—" Those who render our people idle are the first to ridicule them for that idleness, and to ridicule them without a cause. National characteristics are always unjust, as there never was a country that has not produced both good and bad." " They are general assertions, as false as they are illiberal. Irishmen have shown spirit and genius in whatever they have undertaken." " I call upon gentlemen to specify one instance where the people were indolent when the laws of their country protected them in their endeavours." ("Irish Debates," iii., p. 127.) " It is a cant in England," says Mr. O'Connell, "that they (the Irish) are an idle people, but how can that be said when they are to be found seeking employment through every part of the world? They are to be found making roads in Scotland and digging canals in the poisonous marshes of New Orleans." ("Discussion in Dublin Corporation on Repeal of the Union," in 1843, p. 58) The *Times* of the 26th of June, 1845, in an article to which I will refer hereafter, says " The Irishman is disposed to work."

tempted as much as others to let their farms on the
terms most profitable to them, the House of Commons
in 1716 resolved unanimously to make an effort for a
general change of system, and to reclaim both people
and country by bringing back and stimulating agriculture.   They passed a vote that covenants which
prohibited the breaking soil with the plough were
impolitic, and should have no binding force.   They
passed heads of a bill, which they recommended with
the utmost earnestness to the consideration of the
English Council, enjoining that for every hundred
acres which any tenant held he should break up and
cultivate five, and, as a further encouragement, that a
trifling bounty should be granted by the Government
on corn grown for exportation.

   "And what did England answer?   England
which was so wisely anxious for the prosperity of the
Protestant interest in Ireland :   England which was
struggling so pathetically to make the Irish peers and
gentlemen understand the things that belonged to
their peace?   The bounty system might or might
not have been well calculated to produce the effect
which Ireland desired.   It was the system which
England herself practised with every industry which
she wished to encourage, and it was not on economic
grounds that the Privy Council rejected a Bill which
they ought rather to have thrust of their own accord
on Irish acceptance.   The real motive was probably
the same which had led to the suppression of the
manufactures—the detestable opinion that to govern

Ireland conveniently Ireland must be kept weak. Although the corn consumed in Ireland had been for many years imported, the English farmers were haunted with a terror of being undersold in their own and foreign markets by a country where labour was cheap. A motive so iniquitous could not be confessed, but the objections which the Council were not ashamed to allege were scarcely less disgraceful to them. The English manufacturers having secured, as they supposed, the monopoly of Irish wool on their own terms, conceived that the whole soil of Ireland ought to be devoted to growing it. The merchants of Tiverton and Bideford had recently memorialised the Crown on the diminution of the number of fleeces which reached them from the Irish ports. They attributed the falling off to the contraband trade between Ireland and France, which shortened their supplies, enhanced the price, and gave the French weavers an advantage over them. Their conjecture, as will be hereafter shown, was perfectly just. The contraband trade, as had been foreseen when the restrictions were imposed, had become enormous. But the Commissioners of the Irish Revenue were unwilling to confess to carelessness. They pretended that the Irish farmers, forgetting their obligations to England, and thinking wickedly only of their own interests, were diminishing their stock of sheep, breaking up the soil, and growing wheat and barley. The allegation, unhappily, was utterly untrue. But the mere rumour of a rise of industry in Ireland created a panic in the commercial circles of England. Although the change existed as yet only in desire, and the sheep-farming, with its attending miseries, was increasing rather than diminishing, Stanhope, Walpole, Sutherland, and the other advisers of the English Crown, met the overtures of the Irish Parliament in a spirit of settled hostility, and, with an infatuation which now appears insanity, determined to keep closed the one remaining avenue by which Ireland could have recovered a gleam of prosperity.

"The heads of the Bill were carried in Ireland without a serious suspicion that it would be received unfavourably. A few scornful members dared to say that England would consent to nothing which would really benefit Ireland, but they were indignantly silenced by the friends of the Government. It was sent over by the Duke of Grafton, with the fullest expectation that it would be returned. He learnt first with great surprise that 'the Tillage Bill was meeting with difficulties.' 'It was a measure,' he said, 'which the gentlemen of the country had very much at heart, as the only way left them to improve their estates while they were under such hard restrictions in point of trade.' 'It would be unkind,' he urged, in a second and more pressing letter, 'to refuse Ireland anything not unreasonable in itself. He conceived the Corn Bill was not of that nature, and therefore earnestly requested his Majesty would be pleased to indulge them in it.'

"Stanhope forwarded in answer a report of the

English Commissioners of Customs, which had the merit of partial candour. 'Corn,' they said, 'is supposed to be at so low a rate in Ireland in comparison with England, that an encouragement to the exportation of it would prejudice the English trade.'

"The Lords Justices returned the conclusive rejoinder that for some years past Ireland had imported large quantities of corn from England, which would have been impossible had her own corn been cheaper. 'They could not help representing,' they said, 'the concern they were under to find that verified which those all along foretold who obstructed the King's affairs, and which his friends had constantly denied, that all the marks they had given of duty and affection would not procure one bill for the benefit of the nation.

"The fact of the importation of corn from England could not be evaded ; but the commercial leaders were possessed with a terror of Irish rivalry which could not be exorcised. The bill was at last transmitted, but a clause had been slipped in empowering the Council to suspend the premiums at their pleasure ; and the House of Commons in disgust refused to take back a measure which had been mutilated into a mockery."*

To take another instance, illustrative of the same

* "English in Ireland,', vol. i., 441—446. The subsequent history of this Bill as related by Mr. Froude is interesting. It became law in 1727, but was practically ineffective. See Lecky's "Eighteenth Century," ii., 248.

D

system, which was in full operation sixty years later.
The heads of a bill were introduced in 1771 to prevent
corn from being wasted in making whisky, and to
put some restraint on the vice of drunkenness, which
was increasing.   This bill was warmly recommended
to the English Privy Council by Townshend, the Lord-
Lieutenant of the day, who said, "the whisky shops
were ruining the peasantry and the workmen.   There
was an earnest and general desire to limit them.   It
will be a loss to the revenue, but it is a very popular
bill, and will give general content and satisfaction
throughout the kingdom." *   "The Whisky Bill,"
says Mr. Froude, "was rejected because the Treasury
could not spare a few thousand pounds which were
levied upon drunkenness." †

It must also be borne in mind that although the
English Parliament could, and, in fact, did, place
prohibitory duties on Irish goods imported into England, it was quite impossible for the Irish Parliament
to exercise the same power.   Bills of such a nature
would, of course, never obtain the sanction of the
English Privy Council, to whom they must have been
submitted.

The difference between the duties on the same
goods when imported from England into Ireland, and
from Ireland into England, were in some cases striking.
"In Ireland," says Mr. Parsons, speaking in the Irish
Parliament in 1784, "no more than 6d. a yard was

* " English in Ireland," vol. ii., 113, 114.
† " English in Ireland," vol. ii., 114.

imposed on the importation of English cloths, while ours in England were charged with a duty of £2 0s. 6d."*

Mr. Pitt, speaking as Prime Minister in the British House of Commons in February, 1785, stated that on most of the manufactures of Ireland prohibitory duties were laid by Great Britain. "They (the Irish) had not," he said, "admitted our commodities totally free from duties; they bore, upon an average, about ten per cent."†

The helplessness of the Irish Parliament during this period is demonstrated by Hely Hutchinson. He states that in 1721, during a period of great distress, the speech from the Throne, and the Addresses to the King and the Lord-Lieutenant declare in the strongest terms the great decay of trade, and the very low and impoverished state to which the country was reduced. "But," he says, "it is a melancholy proof of the desponding state of this kingdom, that no law whatever was then proposed for encouraging trade or manufactures, or, to follow the words of the address, for reviving trade or making us a flourishing people, unless that for amending laws as to butter and tallow casks deserves to be so called. And why? Because it was well understood by both Houses of Parliament that they had no power to remove those restraints which prohibited trade and discouraged manufactures, and that any application for that purpose would at

* "Irish Debates," vol. iii., 132.
† " Parliamentary Register," 17, 255.

D 2

that time have only offended the people on one side of
the Channel, without bringing any relief to those on
the other."*

The Irish Parliament did, however, what they
could. Thus, "in the sessions of 1703, 1705, and
1707, the House of Commons resolved unanimously
that it would greatly conduce to the relief of the poor
and the good of the kingdom, that the inhabitants
thereof should use none other but the manufactures of
this kingdom in their apparel, and the furniture of
their houses ; and in the last of those sessions, the
members engaged their honours to each other that
they would conform to the said resolution." † Many
of their suggestions for the encouragement of home
produce are of extraordinary ingenuity. In 1727, the
Privy Council allowed a bill to become law, entitled
" An Act to encourage the home consumption of wool
by burying in wool only," providing that no person
should be buried "in any stuff or thing other than

---

* "Commercial Restraints," pp. 40—41. Speaking of the great
distress in the years 1740 and 1741, Hely Hutchinson again deplores
the inability of the Irish Parliament to alleviate the misery of the poor.
" They (the Commons) could not have been insensible of the miseries
of their fellow-creatures, many thousands of whom were lost in those
years, some from absolute want and many from disorders occasioned by
bad provisions. Why was no attempt made for their relief? Because
the Commons knew that the evil was out of their reach, and the poor
were not employed because they were discouraged by restrictive laws
from working up the materials of their own country, and that agriculture could not be encouraged when the lower classes of the people were
not enabled by their industry to purchase the produce of the farmer's
labour."—("Commercial Restraints," pp. 47—48.)

† "Commercial Restraints," pp. 210, 211.

what is made of sheep or lambs' wool only."* The custom, now grotesque and unmeaning, but still in vogue in Ireland, of wearing scarfs at funerals, was recommended in the interest of the linen manufacture, and was first introduced in 1729 at the funeral of Mr. Conolly, Speaker of the Irish House of Commons.† So, too, spinning schools were established in every county, and a board of trustees was appointed to watch over the interests of the linen manufacture; "but the utter want of capital, the neglect of the grand juries, the ignorance, poverty, and degradation of the inhabitants, made the attempt to create a new manufacture hopeless." ‡

These efforts of the Irish Parliament, though of little practical effect, demonstrate their keen appreciation of the sufferings around them and their sympathy with the wants and wishes of their people, who were crushed by a system which Mr. Pitt has characterised as one "of cruel and abominable restraint."§

---

* 7 George II. (Irish) c. 13. This Irish Statute was framed on the model of an Act passed by the English Parliament in 1678, providing that all dead bodies should be wrapped in woollen shrouds. Dean Swift warmly approved of this measure which, however, he seemed to think would never pass the Privy Councils. "What," he says, "if we should agree to make burying in woollen a fashion, as our neighbours have made it a law?" Swift's Works (Scott's Ed.), vi., p. 274.

† Finlayson's "Monumental Inscriptions in Christ Church Cathedral, Dublin," p. 27.

‡ Lecky's "Eighteenth Century," vol. ii., 215.

§ "Parliamentary Register," 17, 249. Mr. Lecky pays a high compliment to the exertions of the Irish Parliament to protect the material interests of their country. "During the greater part of the century (18th century) it had little power except that of protesting against laws

Speaking in the English House of Commons in 1785, that statesman bade members "recollect that from the Revolution to a period within the memory of every man who heard him, indeed until these very few years, the system had been that of debarring Ireland from the enjoyment and use of her own resources, to make that kingdom completely subservient to the interests and opulence of this country, without suffering her to share in the bounties of nature, in the industries of her citizens, or making them contribute to the general interests and strength of the empire."*

"No country," says Mr. Lecky, "ever exercised a more complete control over the destinies of another than did England over those of Ireland, for three-quarters of a century after the Revolution. No serious resistance of any kind was attempted. The nation was as passive as clay in the hands of the potter, and it is a circumstance of peculiar aggravation that a large part of the legislation I have recounted was a distinct violation of a solemn treaty.† The commercial legislation which ruined Irish industry, the confiscation of Irish land which demoralised and impoverished the nation, were all directly due to the English Government, and the English Parliament." ‡

"If," says Mr. Froude, "the high persons at the

---

crushing Irish commerce, but what little it could do it appears to have done."—"Leaders of Public Opinion in Ireland," p. 187.

* "Parliamentary Register," 17, 249.

† Mr. Lecky refers doubtless to the Treaty of Limerick.

‡ "Eighteenth Century," vol. ii., 256.

head of the great British Empire had deliberately considered by what means they could condemn Ireland to remain the scandal of their rule, they could have chosen no measures better suited to their end than those which they pursued unrelentingly through three-quarters of a century." *

* "English in Ireland," vol. ii., 213.

CHAPTER IV.

THE IMMEDIATE EFFECTS OF ENGLISH LEGISLA-
TION ON IRISH TRADE.

THE immediate effects produced upon Ireland by the
commercial policy of Great Britain were such as
might reasonably be anticipated from the brief and
necessarily imperfect account I have given of that
system. The best and most energetic members of
the industrial community sought refuge in exile
from a land where honest labour was robbed by
law of its reward. The weaker ones, who were compelled to remain, this terrible system defrauded, impoverished, and degraded. It afflicted every Irishman, whether at home or abroad, with a sense of
intolerable wrong, and created that passionate resentment towards England, which has been transmitted to succeeding generations. "One of the most
obvious consequences," says Mr. Lecky, "was that for
the space of about a century Ireland underwent a
steady process of depletion, most men of energy, ambition, talent, or character being driven from her
shores." * "If the ambition of an Irishman lay in the
paths of manufacture and commerce he was almost
compelled to emigrate, for industrial and commercial

* "Eighteenth Century," vol. ii., 257, 258.

enterprise had been deliberately crushed."* This
legislation, it must be remembered, fell most severely
on the Protestant population of Ireland, although, of
course, it grievously affected every class, and, indeed,
every member of the community.   Twenty thousand
Puritans left Ulster on the destruction of the woollen
trade.† "Until the spell of tyranny was broken, in
1782, annual ship-loads of families poured themselves
out from Belfast and Londonderry.   The resentment
they carried with them continued to burn in their new
homes ; and, in the War of Independence, England
had no fiercer enemies than the great-grandsons of
the Presbyterians who had held Ulster against Tyr-
connel." ‡

At the beginning of the eighteenth century, Mr.
Lecky thinks the population of Ireland slightly exceeded two millions,§ and he adopts the calculation
of a contemporary writer that the woollen manufacture at the time of its suppression afforded employment to 12,000 Protestant families in the metropolis,
and 30,000 dispersed over the rest of the kingdom.‖
We can, therefore, see at a glance how large a fraction
of the entire population of the country were directly
deprived of bread by that measure. Swift, whose
deanery lay in the liberties of Dublin, the principal
seat of the woollen manufacture, and who witnessed

---

* "Eighteenth Century," vol. ii., 259.
† "English in Ireland," vol. i., 435.
‡ "English in Ireland," vol. i., 436.
§ "Eighteenth Century," vol. ii., 255.
‖ "Eighteenth Century," vol. ii., 213.

the results of its suppression, thus writes :—" Three
parts in four of the inhabitants of that district of the
town where I dwell were English manufacturers,
whom either misfortunes in trade, little petty debts
contracted through illness, or the presence of a
numerous family, had driven into our cheap country.
These were employed in working up our worse wool,
while the finest was sent into England. Several of these
had taken the children of the native Irish apprentices
to them who, being humbled by the forfeiture of
upwards of three millions by the Revolution, were
obliged to stoop to a mechanic industry. Upon the
passing of this bill, we were obliged to dismiss thousands of these people from our service. Those who
had settled their affairs returned home, and over-
stocked England with workmen ; those whose debts
were unsatisfied, went to France, Spain, and the
Netherlands, where they met with good encouragement, whereby the natives having got a firm footing
in the trade, being acute fellows, so became as good
workmen as any we have, and supply the foreign
manufacturers with a constant supply of artisans."*

 " Upon the checking the export of our woollen
manufactures," writes Mr. Arthur Dobbs, in 1729,
" and by laying on heavy duties on its being exported
to England in 1699 and 1700, equivalent to a prohibition, most of those who were embarked in it were laid
under a necessity of removing elsewhere ; and, being

* Swift's Works (Scott's Ed.), vol. vii., 195.

piqued at the difficulties they were laid under, many
of the Protestants removed into Germany, and settled
in the Protestant states there, who received them with
open arms. Several Papists at the same time removed into the northern parts of Spain, where they
laid the foundations of a manufacture highly prejudicial to England. Many also of the Protestants
who were embarked with Papists in the woollen
manufacture, removed into France, and settled at
Roan and other parts. Notwithstanding Louis XIV.
had repealed the Edict of Nantes, and forced abroad
the French Protestants into different parts of Europe,
yet these were kindly received by him, had great
encouragement given to them, and were protected in
their religion. From these beginnings they have in
many branches so much improved the woollen manufactures of France, as not only to supply themselves,
but even to vie with the English in the foreign
markets ; and by their correspondence they have laid
the foundation for the running of wool thither both
from England and Ireland, highly to the prejudice of
Britain, which pernicious practice is still carried on in
spite of all the care and precaution made use of to
discountenance and prevent it. Thus a check is put
upon the sale of our woollen manufactures abroad,
which would have given employment to all the
industrious poor both of Britain and Ireland,
had not our manufacturers been forced away into
France, Spain, and Germany, where they are now
so improved as in great measure to supply them-

selves with many sorts they formerly had from
England." *

In 1773 the Irish House of Commons "had to
hear from the Linen Board that 'many thousands
of the best manufacturers and weavers, with their
families, had gone to seek their bread in America, and
thousands were preparing to follow.' Again a committee was appointed to inquire. This time the blame
was laid on England, which had broken the linen compact, given bounties to Lancashire mill-owners, which
Belfast was not allowed to share, and in 'jealousy of
Irish manufactures,' had laid duties on Irish sail-cloth
contrary to express stipulation. The accusation, as
the reader knows, was true." † "If," wrote Mr.
Newenham, in 1805, "we said that, during fifty
years of the last century, the average annual emigration to America and the West Indies amounted to
4,000, and consequently that in that space of time
200,000 had emigrated to the British Plantations, I
am disposed to think we should rather fall short of
than exceed the truth." ‡

It would be easy to adduce further evidence of the
extent of this emigration caused by the destruction of
Irish manufactures and its results. The speech, however, of the Right Hon. Luke Gardiner, delivered in
the Irish House of Commons on the 2nd of April,

* " An Essay upon the Trade of Ireland "—" Tracts and Treatises "
(Ireland), 2, p. 335-6.
† " English in Ireland," vol. ii., 137.
‡ Newenham on " Population," p. 60. This remark is quoted by
Mr. Lecky.

1784, is noteworthy. Having described the destruction of the woollen trade, which was initiated by the Irish Act laying it under temporary prohibitions, passed by "a corrupt majority in this House;" the consequent emigration of the manufacturers, their favourable reception in foreign countries, and especially in France, who, availing herself of their industry, was enabled, not only "to rival Great Britain, but to undersell her in every market in Europe," the speaker proceeded thus—

"England, from unhappy experience, is convinced of the pernicious effects of her impolicy. The emigration of the Irish manufacturers in the reign of King William is not the only instance that has taught that nation the ruinous effects of restrictive laws. Our own remembrance has furnished a sad instance of the truth of this assertion—furnished it in the American war. America was lost by Irish emigrants. These emigrations are fresh in the recollection of every gentleman in this House; and when the unhappy differences took place, I am assured, from the best authority, that the major part of the American army was composed of Irish, and that the Irish language was as commonly spoken in the American ranks as English. I am also informed it was their valour determined the conquest; so that England not only lost a principal protection of her woollen trade, but also had America detached from her by force of Irish emigrants "*

* "Irish Debates," vol. iii., 132.

The weaker and more defenceless members of the Irish industrial community were forced by circumstances to remain at home, and were accordingly exposed to the sufferings entailed by this policy of unenlightened selfishness and exasperation.

The following extracts, taken from a mass of contemporaneous documents, will give some idea of their condition.

" From the time," says Hely Hutchinson, " of this prohibition [of the woollen manufactures] no Parliament was held in Ireland till the year 1703. Five years were suffered to elapse before any opportunity was given to apply a remedy to the many evils which such a prohibition must necessarily have occasioned. The linen trade was then not thoroughly established in Ireland ; the woollen manufacture was the staple trade, and wool the principal material of that kingdom. The consequences of the prohibition appear in the session of 1713. The Commons lay before Queen Anne a most affecting representation containing, to use their own words, 'a true state of our deplorable condition,' protesting that no groundless discontent was the motive for that application, but a deep sense of the evil state of their country, and of the further mischiefs they have reason to fear will fall upon it if not timely prevented. They set forth the vast decay and loss of its trade, its being almost exhausted of coin that they are hindered from earning their livelihoods, and from maintaining their own manufactures ; that their poor have thereby become very

numerous ; that great numbers of Protestant families
have been constrained to remove out of the kingdom,
as well into Scotland as into the dominions of foreign
princes and states ; and that their foreign trade and
its returns are under such restrictions and discourage-
ments as to be then become in a manner imprac-
ticable, although that kingdom had by its blood and
treasure contributed to secure the plantation trade to
the people of England.

"In a further Address to the Queen, laid before the
Duke of Ormonde, then Lord-Lieutenant, by the
House, with its Speaker, they mention the distressed
condition of that kingdom, and more especially of the
industrious Protestants, by the almost total loss of
trade and decay of their manufactures, and, to pre-
serve the country from utter ruin, apply for liberty
to export their linen manufactures to the Plantations.

"In a subsequent part of this session the Commons resolve that, by reason of the great decay
of trade and discouragement of the manufactures of
this kingdom, many poor tradesmen were reduced to
extreme want and beggary. This resolution was agreed
to *nem. con.*, and the Speaker, Mr. Broderick, then
his Majesty's Solicitor-General, and afterwards Lord
Chancellor, in his speech at the end of the session,
informs the Lord-Lieutenant that 'the representation
of the Commons was, as to the matters contained in it,
the unanimous voice and consent of a very full House,
and that the soft and gentle tones used by the Commons in laying the distressed condition of the

kingdom before his Majesty, showed that their complaints proceeded not from querulousness, but from a necessity of seeking redress.'" *

In his proposal for the use of Irish manufactures, which was published in 1720, Dean Swift says: "The Scripture tells us that oppression makes a wise man mad, therefore, consequently speaking, the reason why some men are not mad is because they are not wise. However, it were to be wished that oppression would in time teach a little wisdom to fools."† "Whoever travels in this country and observes the face of nature, and the faces and habits and dwellings of the natives, will hardly think himself in a land where law, religion, or common humanity is professed."‡ Nicholson, an Englishman, translated from the Bishopric of Carlisle to that of Derry, in a letter to the Archbishop of Canterbury, written in the same year, gives a similar account of the prevailing destitution: "Never did I behold in Picardy, Westphalia, and Scotland, such dismal marks of hunger and want as appeared in the countenances of most of the poor creatures I met with on the road." He states that one of his carriage horses having been killed by accident, it was surrounded by "fifty or sixty famished cottagers, struggling desperately to obtain a morsel of flesh for themselves and their children." § Swift, writing in 1727, says:

* "Commercial Restraints," pp. 24—27.
† Swift's Works (Scott's Edition), vol. vi., p. 277.
‡ Swift's Works (Scott's Edition), vol. vi., 281, 282.
§ "England in the Eighteenth Century," vol. ii., 216.

"The conveniency of ports and harbours, which nature has bestowed so liberally on this country, is of no more use to us than a beautiful prospect to a man shut up in a dungeon."* "Ireland is the only kingdom I ever heard of, either in ancient or modern story, which was denied the liberty of exporting their native commodities and manufactures wherever they pleased, except to countries at war with their own Prince or State ; yet this privilege, by the mere superiority of power, is refused us in the most momentous parts of our commerce ; besides an Act of Navigation, to which we never consented, pinned down upon us, rigorously executed, and a thousand other unexampled circumstances, as grievous as they are invidious to mention."† "If we do flourish it must be against every law of nature and reason, like the thorn of Glastonbury, that blossoms in the midst of the winter."‡ "The miserable dress, diet, and dwelling of the people, the general desolation in most parts of the kingdom, the old seats of the nobility in ruins, and no new ones in their stead, the families of farmers, who pay great rents, living in filth and nastiness, upon butter-milk and potatoes, without a shoe or stocking to their feet, or a house so convenient as an English hogsty to receive them. These, indeed, may be comfortable sights to an English spectator, who comes for a short time only to learn the language,

* Swift's Works (Scott's Edition), vol. vii., p. 115.
† *Ibid.*, pp. 115, 116.
‡ *Ibid.*, p. 118.

E

and returns back to his own country whence he finds
all his wealth transmitted.

<blockquote>" Nostra miseria magna est.</blockquote>

There is not one argument used to prove the riches
of Ireland which is not a logical demonstration of its
poverty." * "Ireland is the poorest of all civilised
countries, with every advantage to make it one of the
richest." †

"The great scarcity of corn," says Hely Hutchinson, "had been so universal in this kingdom in the
years 1728 and 1729 as to expose thousands of families to the utmost necessities, and even to the danger
of famine, many artificers and housekeepers having
been obliged to beg for bread in the streets of
Dublin." ‡   This is probably the distress to which
Swift, writing in 1729, alludes : " Our present calamities are not to be represented.   You can have no
notion of them without beholding them.   Numbers of
miserable objects crowd our doors, begging us to take
their wares at any price to prevent their families from
immediate starving." §

"In twenty years," says Mr. Lecky, "there were
at least three or four of absolute famine."||

The writer of a pamphlet entitled "The Groans of

* Swift's Works (Scott's Edition), vol. vii., pp. 118, 119.
† *Ibid.*, p. 135.
‡ "Commercial Restraints," p. 44.
§ Swift's Works (Scott's Edition), vol. vii., p. 199.
|| "Eighteenth Century," vol. ii., p. 218.

Ireland in a Letter to a Member of Parliament," published in Dublin in 1741, thus begins :—

"I have been absent from this country for some years, and on my return to it last summer found it the most miserable scene of universal distress that I ever read of in history.

"Want and misery in every face, the rich unable, almost as they were unwilling, to relieve the poor ; the roads spread with dead and dying bodies ; mankind of the colour of the docks and nettles which they fed on ; two or three, sometimes more, on a car going to the grave for want of bearers to carry them, and many buried only in the fields and ditches where they perished. This universal scarcity was ensued by malignant fevers, which swept off multitudes of all sorts ; whole villages were laid waste by want and sickness and death in various shapes, and scarce a house in the whole island escaped from tears and mourning.

"It were to be wished, Sir, that some curious enquirer had made a calculation of the numbers lost in this terrible calamity. If one for every house in the kingdom died (and that is very probable, when we consider that whole families and villages were swept off in many parts together), the loss must have been upwards of 400,000 souls. If but one for every other house (and it was certainly more), 200,000 perished— a loss too great for this ill-peopled country to bear and the more grievous as the loss was mostly of the grown-up part of the working people."

E 2

The writer then proceeds to emphasise the fact to which Swift had previously directed attention : that Irish famines are *artificial.*

"Sir, — When a stranger travels through this country and beholds its wide extended and fertile plains, its great flocks of sheep and black cattle, and all its natural wealth and conveniences for tillage, manufactures, and trade, he must be astonished that such misery and want could possibly be felt by its inhabitants ; but you, who know the Constitution and are acquainted with its weaknesses, can easily see the reason." *

Writing in the year 1779, Hely Hutchinson says, " In this and the last year about twenty thousand manufacturers in this metropolis were reduced to

---

* The resemblance between this account of the famine of 1740 and the account of the condition of Ireland in the June preceding the last Irish Famine, as given by the *Times,* is striking. In an article of the 26th June, 1845, that paper says—"The facts of Irish destitution are ridiculously simple. They are almost too commonplace to be told. The people have not enough to eat. They are suffering a real, though an artificial, famine. Nature does her duty. The land is fruitful enough. Nor can it be fairly said that man is wanting. The Irishman is disposed to work. In fact, man and Nature together do produce abundantly. The island is full and overflowing with human food. But something ever interposes between the hungry mouth and the ample banquet. The famished victim of a mysterious sentence stretches out his hand to the viands which his own industry has placed before his eyes, but no sooner are they touched than they fly. A perpetual decree of *sic vos non nobis* condemns him to toil without enjoyment. Social atrophy drains off the vital juices of the nation." Mr. Lecky quotes from " The Groans of Ireland," a copy of which he found in the Halliday Collection of Pamphlets in the Irish Academy (" Eighteenth Century," vol. ii., p. 218). My attention was attracted by the reference, and, on inquiry, I ascertained that there were several copies of this pamphlet in the Library of the King's Inns.

beggary for want of employment; they were for a
considerable length of time supported by alms; a
part of the contribution came from England, and this
assistance was much wanting, from the general distress
of all ranks of people in this country. Public and
private credit are annihilated." * Again, "A country
will sooner recover from the miseries and devastation
occasioned by war, invasion, rebellion, and massacre,
than from laws restraining the commerce, discouraging the manufactures, fettering the industry, and,
above all, breaking the spirits of the people." † He
thus summarises the effects of the eighty years'
restrictive legislation, between the destruction of the
woollen trade in 1699 and 1779, the date at which he
was writing. "Can the history of any other fruitful
country on the globe, enjoying peace for fourscore
years, and not visited by plague or pestilence, produce so many recorded instances of the poverty and
wretchedness, and of the reiterated want and misery
of the lower orders of the people? There is no such
example in ancient or modern story. If the ineffec-
tual endeavours by the representatives of those poor
people to give them employment or food had not
left sufficient memorials of their wretchedness, if
their habitations, apparel, and food were not sufficient
proofs, I should appeal to the human countenance
for my voucher, and rest the evidence on that hope-

---

* " Commercial Restraints," p. 2.
† *Ibid.*, pp. 31, 32.

less despondency that hangs on the brow of unemployed industry." *

Such were the more striking effects of this pernicious legislation. Its remoter consequences were likewise disastrous. Crime and outrage were promoted by the suppression of national industry. "In the year 1762," says Hely Hutchinson, "a new evil made its appearance, which all the exertions of the Government and of the Legislature have not since been able to eradicate. I mean the risings of the White Boys. They appear in those parts of the kingdom where manufactures are not established, and are a proof of the poverty and want of employment of the lower classes of our people."† Then again, this system divorced law from public opinion. Sir Henry Maine has well observed, that social necessities and social opinion are always more or less in advance of law, and that the greater or less happiness of a nation depends on the degree of promptitude with which the gulf between them is narrowed.‡ In Ireland that gulf was deliberately widened; and the people learned, with good reason, to regard the law, not as a protector, but as a plunderer of their rightful gains, and as an agency to make havoc of their industry. "When England," says Mr. Froude, "in defence of her monopolies, thought proper to lay restrictions on the Irish woollen trade, it was foretold

* " Commercial Restraints," pp. 78, 79.
† *Ibid.*, p. 69.
‡ " Ancient Law," p. 24.

that the inevitable result would be an enormous development of smuggling."* "The entire nation, high and low, was enlisted in an organised confederacy against the law. Distinctions of creed were obliterated, and resistance to law became a bond of union between Catholic and Protestant, Irish Celt and English colonist."† Hely Hutchinson, in a paper laid before Lord Buckinghamshire, in July, 1779, places this matter in a clear light. "You have forced us into an illicit commerce, and our very existence depends now upon it. Ireland has paid Great Britain for eleven years past double the sum that she collects from the whole world in all the trade which Great Britain allows her, a fact not to be paralleled in the history of the world. Whence did the money come? But one answer is possible. It came from the contraband trade, and surely it is madness to suffer an important part of the empire to continue in that condition. You defeat your own objects." ‡

Again, this system embittered the relations between landlord and tenant in Ireland by raising unduly the creation of farms, the cultivation of the soil being the only industrial resource left to the people. "Rents," says Mr. Lecky, "were regulated by competition ; but it was competition between a half starving population, who had no other resource except the soil, and were

* " English in Ireland," vol. i., p. 497.
† *Ibid.*, p. 500.
‡ *Ibid.*, vol. ii., p. 247.

prepared to promise anything rather than be deprived of it.*   The mass of the people," the same writer continues, " became cottiers, because it was impossible to gain a livelihood as agricultural labourers or in mechanical pursuits.   This impossibility was due to the extreme paucity of circulating capital, and may be chiefly traced to the destruction of Irish manufactures and to the absence of a considerable class of resident landlords, who would naturally give employment to the poor." †

Such were some of the more immediate effects upon Ireland of the commercial arrangements of Great Britain.   That system was thus described in the Irish House of Commons in October, 1779, by Hussey Burgh, who then held the office of Prime Serjeant, and afterwards became Lord Chief Baron of the Court of Exchequer.   " The usurped authority of a foreign Parliament has kept up the most wicked laws that a jealous, monopolising, ungrateful spirit could desire, to restrain the bounty of Providence and enslave a nation whose inhabitants are recorded to be a brave, loyal, generous people ; by the English code of laws, to answer the most sordid views, they have been treated with a savage cruelty ; the words penalty, punishment, and Ireland are synonymous ; they are marked in blood on the margin of their statutes, and though time may have softened the calamities of the nation, the baneful and destructive influence of those

---

* " Eighteenth Century," vol. ii., p. 241.
† *Ibid.*, p. 243.

laws have borne her down to a state of Egyptian bondage. The English have sowed their laws like serpents' teeth ; they have sprung up as armed men." *

Few will be disposed to disagree with Mr. Froude in his estimate of the effects of this policy. "By a curious combination this system worked the extremity of mischief, commercially, socially, and politically." †

* "MacNevin's Volunteers," p. 117. Mr. Froude well observes that these memorable words "had nothing to do with penal laws, and related entirely to the restrictions on trade." "English in Ireland," vol. ii., p. 264.

† "English in Ireland," vol. i., p. 502. In these pages I have designedly refrained from referring to the Penal Code. I have confined myself entirely to a recital of the leading features of the restrictions imposed by England on Irish trade. It is, in my opinion, impossible to estimate, in distinct scales, the evils done by these terrible agencies. They acted and re-acted on each other, and affected not merely the special objects of legislation, but more or less directly every interest in the community. The able writer of a pamphlet, "Irish Wool and Woollens," to which I have frequently referred, says :—" Possibly the laws that annihilated the wool trade wrought more destruction than the legislation that aimed at stamping out the Catholic faith, for the trade Acts snatched bread from the mouth, filched hope from the heart, and wrenched power from the hands of the industrial sections of the community." (p. 43.) From this opinion I am constrained to differ. Speaking as a Protestant, I have no hesitation in saying that the injuries inflicted on Ireland by the Penal Code exceeded the injuries inflicted on her by the trade regulations. "Well," says the Rev. Canon MacColl, "may Mr. Matthew Arnold speak of that Penal Code, of which the monstrosity is not half known to Englishmen, and may be studied by them with profit." ("Arguments For and Against Home Rule," p. 60.)

CHAPTER V.

THE IRISH VOLUNTEER MOVEMENT AND FREE TRADE.

THE nature and effects of the Irish Volunteer Movement have often been stated and explained. I can only touch upon this movement in a very cursory manner, confining myself strictly to its bearings on the commercial arrangements between Great Britain and Ireland. A very superficial study of Irish history will show that national movements have a tendency to grow out of controversies on trade and mercantile questions. Thus the destruction of the woollen trade by the English Parliament led Irish politicians to question the right of that Parliament to legislate for Ireland at all. William Molyneux, in his celebrated "Case of Ireland stated," published in 1698, asks, "Shall we of this kingdom be denied the birthright of every free-born English subject by having laws imposed on us when we are neither personally nor representatively present?" * "That book," says Chief Justice Whiteside, "met with a fate which it did not deserve. The English Parliament ordered that it should be burned, and thereby much increased

* "Case of Ireland," p. 105.

the estimation in which it was held in Ireland." *
Thus, too, the agitation against Wood's half-pence,
a purely commercial topic, assumed insensibly a
national complexion. In his fourth Drapier's letter,
Swift changes the controversy into an examination of
Ireland's political condition. " The remedy," he says,
" is wholly in your own hands, and therefore I have
digressed a little in order to refresh and continue that
spirit so seasonably raised among you, and to let you
see that by the laws of God, of nature, and of nations,
and of your country, you are and ought to be as free
a people as your brethren in England." † Swift's
prosecution by the Government of the day and its
failure are well known. Lord Chief Justice Whiteside thus comments on his public conduct. " Had
there been a few in the Irish Parliament possessed of
the originality, energy, honesty, and capacity of Swift,
the management of political affairs and the true
interests of the country would have been speedily
improved instead of being shamefully neglected.
Swift created a public opinion ; Swift inspired hope,
courage, and a spirit of justifiable resistance in the
people ; Swift taught Irishmen they had a country to
love, to raise, and to cherish. No man who recalls
the affectionate respect paid by his countrymen to
Swift while he lived, to his memory when dead, can

---

* Reg. *v.* O'Connell, p. 533. This observation was made by Mr.
(afterwards Chief Justice) Whiteside in his speech in defence of Mr.
(now Sir C. Gavan) Duffy, in the State Trials, 1844.
† Swift's Works (Scott's Edition), vol. vi., p. 448.

impute political ingratitude to be amongst the vices of the Irish people." *

Then, again, besides actively disputing England's right to destroy the trade and manufactures of the country, there was another remedy which lay in the people's own hands. They could, by the exercise of self-control, use Irish manufactures alone.

"England," says Mr. Froude, "might lay a veto on every healthy effort of parliamentary legislation; but England could not touch the self-made laws which the conscience and spirit of the nation might impose upon themselves." Hely Hutchinson has pointed out, that "the not importing goods from England is one of the remedies recommended by the Council of Trade in 1676 for alleviating some distress that was felt at the time; and Sir William Temple, a zealous friend to the trade and manufactures of England, recommends to Lord Essex, then Lord Lieutenant, to introduce, as far as can be, a vein of parsimony throughout the country in all things that are not perfectly the native growths and manufactures. The people of England cannot reasonably object to a conduct of which they have given a memorable example. In 1697 the English House of Lords presented an Address to King William to discourage the use and wearing of all sorts of furniture and cloths not of the growth and manufacture of that kingdom, and beseech him, by his royal example, effectually to encourage the use and wearing of all sorts of furniture

* "Life and Death of the Irish Parliament," p. 89.

and wearing cloths that are the growth of that kingdom or manufactured there ; and King William
assures them that he would give the example to his
subjects, and would endeavour to make it effectually
followed. The reason assigned by the Lords for
this Address was that the trade of the nation had
suffered by the late long and expensive war. But it
does not appear that there was any pressing necessity
at the time, or that their manufacturers were starving
for want of employment.

"Common sense must discover to every man that
when foreign trade is restrained, discouraged, or prevented in any country, and where that country has
the materials for manufactures, a fruitful soil, and
numerous inhabitants, the home trade is its best
resource. If this is thought by men of great knowledge to be the most valuable of all trades, because it
makes the speediest and surest returns, and because
it increases at the same time two capitals in the same
country, there is no nation on the globe whose wealth,
population, strength, and happiness would be promoted by such a trade in a greater degree than ours." *

The author of the "Commercial Restraints" was a
barrister of great eminence, who had been Prime
Serjeant, was a member of the Irish Privy Council,
Principal Secretary of State, and Provost of Trinity
College, and a distinguished member of the Irish Parliament. This book, however, obtained a reception
similar to that accorded to the " Case of Ireland," and

* " Commercial Restraints," pp. 211—213.

the fourth Drapier's letter.   In the fly-leaf of the copy in the Library of the Honourable Society of the King's Inns, which I have utilised in arranging this treatise, there are the following observations :—— " Of this remarkable book see the *Times* of February 14, 1846.   Extract of a letter of Sir Valentine Blake, M.P. for Galway, in which he says, ' that immediately after its publication it was suppressed, and burned by the common hangman, and that Mr. Flood, in his place in the House of Commons, said he would give one thousand pounds for a copy, and that the libraries of all the three branches of the Legislature could not procure one copy of this valuable work.' "   The editor of a new edition tells us that there are two copies of the work in the Library of Trinity College, Dublin, both of which have been recently obtained, and from one of them the reprint is taken.*   When Hely Hutchinson, in 1779, advocated "the necessity of using our own manufactures," he stated with accuracy that such arguments, though never so universal as at that time, were no new idea in Ireland. It had been recommended half a century before by Swift, and the celebrated Bishop Berkeley.   " I heard," said Swift, writing in 1720, "the late Archbishop of Tuam (Dr. John Vesey) make a pleasant observation that Ireland would never be happy till a law was made for burning everything that came from

---

* "Commercial Restraints," re-edited, with sketch of the author's life, introduction, notes, and index, by Rev. W. G. Carroll, M.A. Dublin : M. H. Gill & Son.

England, except their people and their coals."* Again, in 1727, he says, "The directions to Ireland are very short and simple, to encourage agriculture and home consumption, and utterly discard all importations that are not absolutely necessary for health or life." † Bishop Berkeley, in the "Querist," published in 1731, asks these questions, which show clearly his views :— "Whether there be upon the earth any Christian or civilised people so beggarly wretched or destitute as the common Irish? Whether, nevertheless, there is any other people whose wants may be more easily supplied from home?"‡ This advice was acted on by the Irish people "after fifty years of expectation." "A great figure," says Chief Justice Whiteside, "now appears upon the stage of public life—Henry Grattan, who took his seat for Charlemont in December, 1775, and began his splendid, though chequered career. The condition of Ireland at this epoch was deplorable. Her industry was shackled, her trade was paralysed, her landed interest was depressed, her exchequer empty, her pension list enormous, her shores undefended, her army withdrawn. The policy and maxims of Swift were revived, a spirit of discontent and a spirit of independence pervaded the nation ; the colonies had revolted, republican ideas were afloat in the world, and Ireland was menaced with invasion. The Government, on being applied to for troops,

---

* Swift's Works (Scott's Edition), vol. vi., p. 275.
† *Ibid.*, vol. vii., p. 182.
‡ "Tracts and Treatises" (Ireland), 2, p. 161.

declared they had none to spare, and that Ireland must protect herself. The Volunteer Movement then commenced, and, to the amazement of ministers, they soon stood face to face with an armed nation." *

Mr. Froude draws this picture of the condition of Ireland in 1779. "The grand juries represented that the fields and highways were filled with crowds of wretched beings half naked and starving. Foreign markets were closed to them. The home market was destroyed by internal distress, and the poor artisans who had supported themselves by weaving were without work and without food. They had bought English goods as long as they had the means to buy them. Now in their time of dire distress they had hoped the English Parliament would be their friend. They learnt with pain and surprise that the only boon which could give them relief was still withheld. They besought the king to interpose in their favour, and procure them leave to export and sell at least the coarse frieze blankets and flannels, which the peasants' wives and children produced in their cabins. Eloquence and entreaty were alike in vain. The English Parliament, though compelled at least to listen to the truth, could not yet bend itself to act upon it. The House of Commons still refused to open the woollen trade in whole or in part, and Ireland, now desperate and determined, and treading ominously in the steps of America, adopted the measures which long before had been recommended by Swift, and resolved to

* "Life and Death of the Irish Parliament," p. 125.

exclude from the Irish market every article of British manufacture which could be produced at home.*

The Earl of Shelburne, speaking in the British House of Lords on the 1st of December, 1779, thus described the attitude of Ireland :—

"Ireland disclaimed any connection with Great Britain, she instantly put herself in a condition of defence against her foreign enemies ; oppressed at one time by England, and at length reduced to a state of calamity and distress experienced by no other country that ever existed, unless visited by war or famine, and perceiving that all prospect of justice or relief was in a manner finally closed, and that she must perish or work out her own salvation, she united as one man to rescue herself from that approaching destruction which seemed to await her. The people instantly armed themselves and the numbers armed soon increased to upwards of 40,000 men, and were daily augmenting. This most formidable body was not composed of mercenaries, who had little or no interest in the issue, but of the nobility, gentry, merchants, citizens, and respectable yeomanry, men able and willing to devote their time and part of their property to the defence of the whole and the protection and security of their country. The Government had been abdicated and the people resumed the powers vested in it, and in doing so were fully authorised by every principle of the Constitution, and every motive of self-preservation, and whenever they should again delegate their inherent power they

* "English in Ireland," ii. 239, 240.

F

firmly and wisely determined to have it so regulated
and placed upon so large and liberal a basis that they
should not be liable to suffer from the same oppression in time to come, nor feel the fatal effects and
complicated evils of maladministration, of calamity
without hope of redress, or of iron-handed power
without protection.   ·

"To prove that these were the declared and real
sentiments of the whole Irish nation, he should not
dwell upon this or that particular circumstance, upon
the resolutions of country or town meetings, upon the
language of the associations, upon the general pre-
valent spirit of all descriptions of men of all religions ;
matters of this kind, however true or manifest, were
subject to and might admit of controversy. He would
solely confine himself to a passage contained in a
State paper, he meant the Address of both Houses of
the Irish Parliament, declaring that nothing but the
granting the kingdom a 'free trade' could save it
from certain ruin.   Here was the united voice of the
country conveyed through its proper constitutional
organs, both Houses of Parliament, to his Majesty,
against which there was but one dissentient voice in
the Houses, not a second, he believed, in the whole
kingdom.   Church of England men and Roman
Catholics, Dissenters, and sections of all denomina-
tions, Whigs and Tories, if any such were to be found
in Ireland, placemen, pensioners, and county gentlemen, Englishmen by birth, in short, every man in
and out of the House, except the single instance men-

tioned, had all united in a single opinion that nothing would relieve the country short of a free trade."*

His lordship proceeds to explain the meaning of the expression "free trade," which was used in a sense different from the modern acceptation of that term :—

"A free trade, he was well persuaded, by no means imported an equal trade. He had many public and private reasons to think so. A free trade imported, in his opinion, an unrestrained trade to every part of the world, independent of the control, regulation, or interference of the British Legislature. It was not a speculative proposition, confined to theory or mere matter of argument ; the people of Ireland had explained the context, if any ambiguity called for such an explanation ; he received accounts from Ireland that a trade was opened between the northern part of Ireland and North America with the privity of Congress, and indemnification from capture by our enemies ; that provision ships had sailed to the same place—nay, more, that Doctor Franklyn, the American Minister at Paris, had been furnished with full power to treat with Ireland upon regulations of commerce and mutual interest and support, and that whether or not any such treaty should take place, the mutual interests of both countries, their very near affinity in blood, and their established intercourse, cemented further by the general advantages arising from an

* The dissentient voice was that of Sir R. Heron, Secretary to the Lord-Lieutenant.

open and unrestrained trade between them, would necessarily perfect what had already actually begun."*

Mr. Lecky thus accurately and distinctly describes the nature of the commercial arrangements under which Ireland obtained the limited free trade which she enjoyed, with some modifications, till the Union :—

"The fear of bankruptcy in Ireland; the non-importation agreements, which were beginning to tell upon English industries; the threatening aspect of an armed body, which already counted more than 40,000 men ; the determined and unanimous attitude of the Irish Parliament ; the prediction of the Lord-Lieutenant that all future military grants in Ireland depended upon his (Lord North's) course ; the danger that England, in the midst of a great and disastrous war, should be left absolutely without a friend, all weighed upon his mind ; and at the close of 1779, and in the beginning of 1780, a series of measures was carried in England which exceeded the utmost that a few years before the most sanguine Irishman could have either expected or demanded. The Acts which prohibited the Irish from exporting their woollen manufactures and their glass were wholly repealed, and the great trade of the colonies was freely thrown open to them. It was enacted that all goods that might be legally imported from the British settlements in America and Africa to Great Britain, may be in

* " Parliamentary Debates," 14, pp. 83—85.

like manner imported directly from those settlements into Ireland, and that all goods which may
be legally exported from Great Britain into those
settlements may in like manner be exported from
Ireland, on the sole condition that duties equal to
those in British ports be imposed by the Irish
Parliament on the goods and exports of Ireland.
The Acts which prohibited carrying gold and silver
into Ireland were repealed. The Irish were allowed
to import foreign hops. They were allowed to
become members of the Turkey Company, and to
carry on a direct trade between Ireland and the
Levant Sea.*

"Thus fell to the ground that great system of
commercial restriction which began under Charles II.,
which under William III. acquired a crushing severity,
and which had received several additional clauses in
the succeeding reigns. The measures of Lord North,
though obviously due in a great measure to intimida-
tion and extreme necessity, were at least largely,
wisely, and generously conceived, and they were the
main sources of whatever material prosperity Ireland
enjoyed during the next twenty years. The English
Parliament had been accustomed to grant a small
bounty—rising in the best years to £13,000—on the
importation into England of the plainer kinds of
Irish linen. After the immense concessions made to
Irish trade, no one could have complained if this
bounty had been withdrawn, but North determined to

* 20 Geo. III. (Eng.), cc. 6, 10, 18.

continue it. He showed that it had been of real use
to the Irish linen manufacture, and he strongly main-
tained that the prosperity of Ireland must ultimately
prove a blessing to England."*

Speaking at the Guildhall in Bristol in 1780,
Edmund Burke thus described the concessions to
Ireland and the series of circumstances to which these
measures owed their origin :—

"The whole kingdom of Ireland was instantly in
a flame. Threatened by foreigners, and, as they
thought, insulted by England, they resolved at once
to resist the power of France and to cast off yours.
As for us, we were able neither to protect nor to
restrain them. Forty thousand men were raised and
disciplined without commission from the Crown ; two
illegal armies were seen with banners displayed
at the same time and in the same country. No
executive magistrate, no judicature in Ireland, would
acknowledge the legality of the army which bore the
King's commission, and no law or appearance of law
authorised the army commissioned by itself. In this
unexampled state of things, which the least error, the
least trespass on our part would have hurried down
the precipice into an abyss of blood and confusion,
the people of Ireland demanded a freedom of trade
with arms in their hands. They interdict all commerce between the two nations ; they deny all new

* "Eighteenth Century," iv. 500, 501.   Some commercial concessions which were, however, manifestly insufficient, had been previously
granted. See "Eighteenth Century," iv., pp. 429, 430, 451.

Supply in the House of Commons, although in time of war ; they stint the trust of the old revenue given for two years to all the King's predecessors to six months. The British Parliament, in a former session frightened into a limited concession by the menaces of Ireland, frightened out of it by the menaces of England, were now frightened back again, and made an universal surrender of all that had been thought the peculiar, reserved, uncommunicable rights of England—the exclusive commerce of America, of Africa, of the West Indies, all the enumerations of the Acts of Navigation, all the manufactures—iron, glass, even the sacred fleece itself—all went together. No reserve, no exception, no debate, no discussion. A sudden light broke in upon us all. It broke in, not through well-contrived and well-disposed windows, but through flaws and breaches, through the yawning chasms of our ruin. We were taught wisdom by humiliation. No town in England presumed to have a prejudice or dared to mutter a petition. What was worse, the whole Parliament of England, which retained authority for nothing but surrenders, was despoiled of every shadow of its superintendence. It was, without any qualification, denied in theory as it had been trampled upon in practice."*

"The chain," says Mr. Froude, "was allowed to remain till it was broken by the revolt of the American colonies, and Ireland was to learn the

* Edmund Burke on "Irish Affairs," edited by M. Arnold, pp. 129, 130.

deadly lesson that her real wrongs would receive attention only when England was compelled to remember them through fear."*

The commercial privileges thus obtained would have been practically valueless unless accompanied with legislative independence. I have explained the system by which measures proposed by the Irish Parliament were robbed of their efficiency by the action of the English and Irish Privy Councils. " To prevent," says Mr. Froude, " the Irish Parliament from being troublesome, it was chained by Poynings' Act ; and when the Parliament was recalcitrant, laws were passed by England over its head." At this time the English Privy Council actively exercised its influence on the commercial legislation of the Irish Parliament. " The business of sugar-refining had recently taken great head in Ireland, and the Irish Parliament sought to defend it against the English monopoly by an import duty on refined sugar ; while they sought to give it a fair stimulus by admitting raw sugar at a low rate. This the Privy Council reversed, reducing the duty on refined sugar 20 per cent. under the drawback allowed in England to the English refiner on export, and thereby giving the latter a virtual premium to that amount, and also increasing the duty on the raw sugar. The time was ill-chosen for further invasions on Irish rights."† " Several minor circumstances concurred to exasperate the Irish people still

* "English in Ireland," vol. ii., p. 104.
† " An Argument for Ireland," by J. O'Connell, M.P., p. 171.

further, and to render irrevocable and, soon after, irresistible, their determination to have a free Parliament, without which they said they never could obtain the extension of their trade amongst other benefits sought, nor even be sure of preserving what had been conceded to them."* Chief Justice Whiteside has given, in a few words, this spirited and accurate description of the attainment of Irish legislative independence—"Down went Poynings' Law, useful in its day ; down went the Act of Philip and Mary ; down went the obnoxious statute of George I. ; the Mutiny Bill was limited ; restrictions on Irish trade vanished ; the ports were opened ; the Judges were made irremovable and independent. I cannot join in the usual exultation at the proceedings of the volunteers ; on the contrary, I regret their occurrence. Not that I think the resolutions carried at Dungannon were in themselves unjust ; not that I would hesitate to claim for Ireland all the rights possessed by our English fellow-subjects ; but because all these inestimable advantages were not granted by the wisdom of the Government, through the recognised channel of Parliament, and were carried at the point of the bayonet. The precedent was dangerous. Had Walpole been alive he would have repented his blunder in listening to Primate Boulter, and refusing to be advised by the counsels of Swift. But the deed was done."† On the 16th of April, 1782, in the Irish House

* " An Argument for Ireland," p. 172.
† " Life and Death of the Irish Parliament," p. 126.

of Commons, Grattan thus expressed his high-wrought enthusiasm :—

"I found Ireland on her knees. I watched over her with an eternal solicitude. I have traced her progress from injuries to arms, and from arms to liberty. Spirit of Swift, spirit of Molyneux, your genius has prevailed. Ireland is now a nation. In that new character I hail her, and bowing in her august presence, I say, Esto Perpetua."*

* Grattan's "Speeches," i. 183.

CHAPTER VI.

THE COMMERCIAL ARRANGEMENTS BETWEEN ENGLAND AND IRELAND, 1782–1800.

THE commercial relations between England and Ireland in the interval between 1782 and 1800 should be clearly understood.

Ireland had, by the Acts of 1779 and 1780, obtained the freedom of foreign and colonial trade, both of export and of import.

By an Act of 1793, she had obtained liberty to re-export foreign and colonial goods from her own shores to England.*

She had, by an English Act of the same year, got the illusory privilege of having an eight-hundred-ton East Indiaman to make up a cargo for the East in her ports. But she had not free trade to the East, nor had she the admission to English ports for her goods.† "The practical boon," says Mr. Butt, "that was won for the Irish nation (by the Volunteers), was the right of the Parliament of Ireland to control our own harbours, and to regulate our own trade. Of course the trade of Ireland was subject to the interference which England could

---

* 33 Geo. III. (Eng.), c. 63.
† "An Argument for Ireland," p. 210.

exercise by her dominion over the colonies and dependencies of the Imperial Crown. A law which would have prohibited the exportation of Irish goods either to England or France or Canada, would have been beyond the power of the English Parliament to pass, but it was perfectly competent to that Parliament to prohibit the importation of these goods into England or Canada, just in the same manner as the French Government might have prohibited their importation into France. The English Parliament was the supreme legislature for England and the colonies, and had just the same power of legislating against the importation of Irish products, as they would have had against those of Holland or of France."

Thus stood the Irish Parliament in constitutional position from 1782 until its dissolution.*

England, as we have seen, had laid prohibitory duties on Irish manufactures, whereas Ireland, bound by the chain of Poynings' Law, was unable to protect her own industries. "It was very natural," in the words of Mr. Pitt, "that Ireland, with an independent legislature, should now look for perfect equality."

In 1783 Mr. Griffiths, advocating in the Irish House of Commons the protection of Irish manufacturers, said : " Lord North knew very well when he granted you a free trade that he gave you nothing, or, at most, a useless bauble, and when petitions were delivered against our free trade by several manufacturing towns

* " Irish Federalism," pp. 38, 39.

in England, he assured them in circular letters that
nothing effectual had or should be granted to Ireland." *

The Irish Parliament, however, on obtaining legislative independence, refrained from measures of retaliation in the hope that the commercial relations of
both countries would be settled on a satisfactory basis.

Mr. Pitt, in introducing in the English House of
Commons his celebrated Commercial Propositions for
the regulation of trade between England and Ireland,
thus speaks: "To this moment (February, 1785) no
change had taken place in the intercourse between
Great Britain and Ireland themselves. Some trivial
points, indeed, had been changed, but no considerable
changes had taken place in our manufactures exported
to Ireland, or in theirs imported to England. That,
therefore, which had been done was still believed by
the people of Ireland to be insufficient, and clamours
were excited and suggestions published in Dublin
and elsewhere of putting duties on our products and
manufactures under the name of protecting duties." †

Chief Justice Whiteside thus states summarily the
scope of Mr. Pitt's propositions :—

"It was proposed to allow the importation of the
produce of all other countries through Great Britain
into Ireland, or through Ireland into Great Britain,
without any increase of duty on that account. It
was proposed, as to any article produced or manu-

* "Irish Debates," iii. 133.
† "Parliamentary Register," xvii., p. 250.

factured in Ireland or in England, where the duties
were then different on importation into either country,
to reduce those duties in the kingdom where they
were highest down to the lower scale. And it was
asked from Ireland that when the gross hereditary
revenue should rise above a fixed sum, the surplus
should be appropriated towards the support of the
naval force of the Empire. These propositions passed
through both branches of the Irish Legislature, were
remitted to England, and by Pitt laid before the
British House of Commons. He was immediately
attacked by Fox and the Whigs, aided by Lord
North, who one and all declared themselves the uncom-
promising enemies of free trade. And these factious
men declared that in the interests of the British
manufacturers they could not allow Irish fustians to
be brought into England to ruin English manufacturers. The fustian they affected to fear was nothing
to be compared with the fustian of their speeches.
The enlightened views of the great Conservative
minister were in a measure baffled by the shameful
opposition of Fox, and of his friends in Parliament,
and of thick-headed cotton manufacturers out of the
House. The result was that Pitt was coerced to introduce exceptions and limitations. The eleven propositions grew up to twenty, the additional propositions relating to various subjects, patents, copyrights,
fisheries, colonial produce, navigation laws, the enactment as to which was that whatever navigation laws
were then, or should thereafter be enacted by the

Legislature of Great Britain, should also be enacted
by the Legislature of Ireland ; and in favour of the
old East India Company monopoly, Ireland was de-
barred from all trade beyond the Cape of Good Hope
to the Straits of Magellan." " There seemed to be
nothing hurtful to the pride of Ireland in the affair.
But when Fox found that his great rival defeated
him on the commercial part of the question, he art-
fully, as Lord Stanhope shows, changed his ground
of attack, and availing himself of the limitations
which Pitt had been compelled to introduce into his
original scheme, Fox cried out that this was a breach
of Ireland's newly-granted independence. ' I will
not,' said Fox, with incredible hypocrisy, or with incredible folly, ' I will not barter English commerce for
Irish slavery, this is not the price I would pay, nor
is this the thing I would purchase.' " "When the
twenty propositions of Mr. Pitt were returned to the
Irish Parliament, they encountered a fierce and pro-
tracted opposition. Mr. Grattan's speech has been
extolled as one of his ablest—it is not intemperate.
His chief objection was to the fourth resolution, by
which he said, ' We are to agree to subscribe whatever laws the Parliament (of England) shall subscribe
respecting navigation ; we are to have no legislative
power—then there is an end of your free trade and
of your free Constitution.' He also curiously ob-
jected that the measure was 'an union—an incipient
and a creeping union—a virtual union establishing
one will in the general concerns of commerce and

navigation, and reposing that will in the Parliament
of Great Britain.'"   "Dublin was illuminated, the
people exulted in the abandonment of the scheme."*

"It was not," says Mr. John O'Connell, "till after
a fair experiment and delay that the Irish Parliament,
despairing of getting England to terms by fair means,
commenced retaliation. To this we have the incontestable testimony of the Commissioners of Revenue
Inquiry in 1822, an authority by no means disposed
to be over-favourable to Irish interests or over-anxious
for the credit of the Irish Parliament. In their
fourth report, speaking of the system of restrictions
on English goods and bounties on their own, to
which that Parliament had recourse, they say :

"Ireland was undoubtedly instigated to the adop-
tion of this course by the exclusive spirit of the commercial policy of England. It will be found that
few exceptions in favour of the sister kingdom were
inserted in the list of goods absolutely prohibited to
be imported into this country (England), in which
list all goods made of cotton-wool, every description
of manufactured woollen, silk, and leather, together
with cattle, sheep, malt, stuffs, and other less important articles were at one time comprehended. In
this embarrassing situation of exclusion from the
markets of Great Britain, and deriving little assistance

* "Life and Death of the Irish Parliament," pp. 142—145. Mr.
Morley's account of the part taken by Fox in this transaction is sub-
stantially in accord with that given by Chief Justice Whiteside. See
"English Men of Letters"—"Edmund Burke," by John Morley,
p. 125.

from foreign trade, Ireland had no other course to pursue for the protection of her own industry except that of maintaining, by restrictive duties on the importations from Great Britain, the manufacturing means she possessed for the supply of her own markets." *

That Ireland made a great advance in prosperity in the interval between 1782 and 1800 is in my judgment incontrovertible.

Mr. O'Connell, when conducting his own defence in the State Trials of 1844, thus spoke with reference to this subject :

"I may be asked whether I have proved that the prophecy of Fox was realised—that the prosperity that was promised to Ireland was actually gained by reason of her legislative independence. Now, pray, listen to me ; I shall tell you the evidence by which I shall demonstrate this fact. It is curious that the first of them is from Mr. Pitt, again in the speech he made in 1799 in favour of the resolutions for carrying the Union. If he could have shown that Ireland was in distress and destitution, that her commerce was lessened, that her manufactures were diminished, that she was in a state of suffering and want by reason of, or during the legislative independence of the country, of course he would have made it his topic in support of his case, to show that a separate Legislature had worked badly, and produced calamities and not blessings ; but the fact was too

* " An Argument for Ireland," p. 211.

G

powerful for him. He had ingenuity to avail himself
of the fact, which fact he admitted ; and let us see how
he admitted it. He admitted the prosperity of Ireland, and here was his reasoning. Now, mark it. 'As
Ireland,' he said, 'was so prosperous under her own
Parliament, we can calculate that the amount of her
prosperity will be trebled under a British Legislature.'
He first quoted a speech of Mr. Foster's in 1785, in
these words :—'The exportation of Irish produce to
England amounts to two millions and a half annually,
and the exportation of British produce to Ireland
amounts to one million.' Instead of saying, 'You are
in want and destitution ; unite with England, and you
will be prosperous,' he was driven to admit this :
'Ireland is prosperous now with her own Parliament,
but it will be trebly prosperous when you give up that
Parliament, or have it joined with the Parliament of
England.' So absurd a proposition was never yet
uttered ; but it shows how completely forced he was to
admit Irish prosperity, when no other argument was
left in his power ; but the absurd observation I have
read to you. He gives another quotation from Foster,
in which it is said Britain imports annually £2,500,000
of our products, all, or nearly all, duty free, and we
import a million of hers, and raise a revenue on almost
every article of it. This relates to the year 1785.
Pitt goes on to say : 'But how stands the case now
(1799) ? The trade at this time is infinitely more
advantageous to Ireland. It will be proved from
the documents I hold in my hand—as far as relates to

the mere interchange of manufactures—that the manufactures exported to Ireland from Great Britain in
1797 very little exceeded one million sterling (the
articles of produce amount to nearly the same sum);
whilst Great Britain, on the other hand, imported from
Ireland to the amount of more than three millions in
the manufacture of linen and linen-yarn, and between
two and three millions in provisions and cattle, besides
corn and other articles of produce.' 'That,' said Mr.
Pitt, 'was in 1785, three years after her legislative
independence ; that was the state of Ireland.' You
have seen, gentlemen, that picture. You have heard
that description. You have heard that proof of the
prosperity of Ireland. She then imported little more
than one million's worth of English manufacture; she
exported two and a half millions of linen and linen-
yarn, adding to that the million of other exports.
There is a picture given of her internal prosperity
Recollect that we now (1844) import largely
English manufactures, and that the greatest part
of the price of these manufactures consists of
wages which the manufacturer gives to the
persons who manufacture them. £2,500,000 worth
of linen and linen-yarn were exported, and one
million of other goods. Compare that with the
present state of things. Does not every one of you
know there is scarcely anything now manufactured
in Ireland, that nearly all the manufactures used in
Ireland are imported from England ? I am now
showing the state of Irish prosperity at the time I

G 2

am talking of. I gave you the authority of Foster (no small one) and of Pitt for Irish prosperity during that time. I will give you the authority of another man that was not very friendly to the people of this country—that of Lord Clare. Lord Clare made a speech in 1798, which he subsequently published, and in which I find this remarkable passage, to which I beg leave to direct your particular attention. 'There is not,' said his lordship, 'a nation on the face of the habitable globe which has advanced in cultivation, in manufactures, with the same rapidity in the same period as Ireland' (namely, from 1782 to 1798). That was the way in which Irish legislative independence worked, and I have in support of it the evidence of Pitt, Foster, and Lord Clare ; and Lord Grey, in 1799, talking of Scotland in the same years, says : 'In truth, for a period of more than forty years after the [Scottish] Union, Scotland exhibited no proofs of increased industry and rising wealth.' Lord Grey, in continuation, stated that 'till after 1748 there was no sensible advance of the commerce of Scotland. Several of her manufactures were not established till sixty years after the Union, and her principal branch of manufacture was not set up, I believe, till 1781. The abolition of the heritable jurisdictions was the first great measure that gave an impulse to the spirit of improvement in Scotland. Since that time the prosperity of Scotland has been considerable, but certainly not so great as that of Ireland has been within the same period.'

Lord Plunket, in his speech in 1799, in one of his happiest efforts of oratory, speaks of her as of 'a little island, with a population of four or five millions of people, hardy, gallant, and enthusiastic, possessed of all the means of civilisation, agriculture, and commerce well pursued and understood, a Constitution fully recognised and established, her revenues, her trade, her manufactures thriving beyond her hope, or the example of any other country of her extent, within these few years advancing with a rapidity astonishing even to herself, not complaining of deficiency in these respects, but enjoying and acknowledging her prosperity.'

"Gentlemen of the Jury, I will now direct your attention to such documents as will tend to corroborate the facts contained in those I have already adverted to. You have heard that in 1810 a meeting was held in Dublin to petition the Legislature for a Repeal of the Union. I will read an unconnected passage from a speech delivered by a gentleman belonging to a most respectable house in this city.* It is as follows :—
'Some of us remember this country before we recovered and brought back our Constitution in the year 1782. We are reminded of it by the present period. Then as now our merchants were without trade, our shopkeepers without customers, our workmen without employment ; then as now it became the universal feeling that nothing but the recovery of

* A Mr. Hutton, the head of a great carriage manufactory in Dublin.

our rights could save us. Our rights were recovered, and how soon afterwards, as if by magic, plenty smiled on us, and we soon became prosperous and happy.' Let me next adduce the testimony of a class of citizens who, from their position and the nature of their avocations, were well calculated to supply important evidence on the state of Ireland subsequent to the glorious achievements of 1782. The bankers of Dublin held a meeting on the 18th of December, 1798, at which they passed the following resolutions :—'Resolved, that since the renunciation of the power of Great Britain in 1782 to legislate for Ireland, the commerce and prosperity of this kingdom have eminently increased.' 'Resolved, that we attribute these blessings, under Providence, to the wisdom of the Irish Parliament.' The Guild of Merchants met on the 14th January, 1799, and passed a resolution declaring ' That the commerce of Ireland has increased, and her manufactures improved beyond example, since the independence of this kingdom was restored by the exertions of our countrymen in 1782. Resolved, that we look with abhorrence on any attempt to deprive the people of Ireland of their Parliament, and thereby of their constitutional right and immediate power to legislate for themselves.' I have given abundance of proofs, from extracts I have read, of the prosperity of Ireland under the fostering care of her own Parliament. A Parliamentary document shows that, from 1785 to the period of the Union, the ncrease in the consumption of teas in Ireland was

84 per cent., while it was only 45 per cent. in England. The increase of tobacco in Ireland was 100 per cent., in England 64 ; in wine, in Ireland 74 per cent., in England 52 ; in sugar, 57 per cent. in Ireland, and in England 53 ; in coffee, in Ireland 600 per cent., in England 75. You have this proof of the growing prosperity of Ireland from the most incontestable evidence. No country ever so rapidly improved as Ireland did in that period."*

* " R. *v.* O'Connell," pp. 623—626. This part of Mr. O'Connell's speech is simply an echo of the speech he delivered in 1843 during the discussion in the Dublin Corporation on Repeal of the Union, in which he relied on the same documentary evidence of Ireland's material prosperity between 1782 and 1800. These proofs could easily be multiplied. Thus Mr. Jebb, afterwards a Justice of the Court of King's Bench in Ireland, published a pamphlet in 1798, in which he says: " In the course of fifteen years our commerce, our agriculture, and our manufactures have swelled to an amount that the most sanguine friends of Ireland could not have dared to prognosticate."

CHAPTER VII.

THE COMMERCIAL ARRANGEMENTS BETWEEN ENGLAND AND IRELAND EFFECTED BY THE ACT OF LEGISLATIVE UNION.

THE commercial arrangements effected between England and Ireland at the time of the Union are embodied in the sixth article of the Act of Union. This article provides that in respect of trade and navigation the subjects of Great Britain and Ireland are to be on the same footing from the 1st of January, 1801 ; that there are to be no duties or bounties on the exportation of produce of one country to the other ; that all articles (except certain specified articles scheduled, which were to be subject to certain countervailing duties) the produce of either country are to be imported free from duty ; that articles enumerated in Schedule II. are to be subject for twenty years to the duties therein mentioned ; that the woollen manufacturers are to pay on importation into each country from the other the duties now payable on importation into Ireland ; that the duties on salt, hops, and wools are not to exceed the duties that were then paid on importation into Ireland ; that the duties on calicoes and muslins are to be liable to the duties then payable on these commodities on importation from Great Britain to Ireland till the 5th of January, 1808 ; that after that date these duties are to be reduced to 10 per cent. till January 5th, 1821, and then to cease altogether; that duties on cotton-yarn and cotton-twist are to be liable to the duties then payable on these commodities * till January 5th, 1808; that these duties are to be reduced annually from that date, and on the 5th of January, 1816, to cease altogether; that the produce of either country, subject to internal duty, is, on importation into each country, to be subject to countervailing duty; that the produce of either country exported through the other is to be subject to the same charges as if it had been exported directly from the country producing it; that duties charged on the import of foreign or colonial produce into either country are, on their export to the other, to be drawn back so long as the expenditure of the United Kingdom shall be defrayed by proportional contributions, but that this provision is not to extend to duties on corn.

The Speaker of the Irish Commons—the Right Hon. John Foster (afterwards Lord Oriel)—was the chief among several able opponents of these regulations. In 1799 and in 1800 he made powerful speeches in opposition, and went largely into the subject of the commercial relations of the two countries, and exposed their past and future inequalities and injustices towards Irish interests. His objections to the 6th Article of Union were, briefly, as follows :—

* On importation from Great Britain to Ireland.

" That they lowered all protecting duties that were above 10 per cent. to that amount, and thus exposed the infant manufactures of Ireland (which the Irish Parliament had in latter years begun to protect) to the overwhelming competition of the great capital and long-established skill and ability of England. That no less than seventy articles of our manufacture would thus be injured, and our cotton manufactures in particular, in which we had begun to make most promising advances, would be nearly ruined. That no preference over foreign goods in the British market was given. That the 'new and excessive' duties on salt were made perpetual, those on hops and coals unalterable. That our brewery was left unprotected, etc. etc."

The opponents of the Union drew up a solemn and elaborate protest in order to perpetuate on the records of Parliament, and hand down to posterity, their views on that subject. Lord Corry moved the Protest and Address to the King, which thus speaks of the commercial arrangements proposed and subsequently carried out under the provisions of the Act of Union: "Were all the advantages which without any foundation they have declared that this measure offers, to be its instant and immediate consequence, we do not hesitate to say expressly that we could not harbour the thought of accepting them in exchange for our Parliament, or that we could or would barter our freedom for commerce, or our constitution for revenue ; but the offers are mere impositions, and we state with the firmest confidence that in commerce or

trade their measure confirms no one advantage, nor
can it confirm any, for by your Majesty's gracious
and paternal attention to this your ancient realm of
Ireland, every restriction under which its commerce
laboured has been removed during your Majesty's
auspicious reign, and we are now as free to trade to
all the world as Britain is. In manufactures, any
attempt it makes to offer any benefit which we do not
now enjoy is vain and delusive, and whenever it is to
have effect, that effect will be to our injury. Most of
the duties on imports which operate as protections to
our manufactures, are under its provisions either to be
removed or reduced immediately, and those which
will be reduced are to cease entirely at a limited
time, though many of our manufacturers owe their
existence to the protection of those duties, and
though it is not in the power of human wisdom to
foresee any precise time when they may be able to
thrive without them. Your Majesty's faithful Commons feel more than an ordinary interest in laying
this fact before you, because they have under your
Majesty's approbation raised up and nursed many of
those manufactures, and by so doing have encouraged
much capital to be vested in them, the proprietors of
which are now to be left unprotected, and to be
deprived of the Parliament on whose faith they
embarked themselves, their families, and properties in
the undertaking." *

* Mr. Whiteside read this Protest in his speech in defence of Mr.
C. G. Duffy, in the State Trials, 1844. (" R. v. O'Connell," pp. 528,
529.)

Mr. Pitt could not have been ignorant of the effect which English competition would produce on the infant and practically unprotected manufactures of Ireland. Thus fifteen years previously, when introducing his Commercial Propositions of 1785 in the English House of Commons, he calmed the fears and raised the hopes of the English manufacturers :—

"It was said that our manufactures were all loaded with heavy taxes. It was certainly true, but with that disadvantage they had always been able to triumph over the Irish in their own markets, paying an additional ten per cent. on the importation to Ireland, and all the charges. But the low price of labour was mentioned. Would that enable them to undersell us? Manufacturers thought otherwise—there were great obstacles to the planting of any manufacture. It would require time for arts and capital, and the capital would not increase without the demand also, and in an established manufacture improvement was so rapid as to bid defiance to rivalship."*

The Irish Parliament, in wishing to protect their infant manufactures, were strictly within the lines of modern economic science. Thus Mr. John Stuart Mill speaks of the wisdom of protecting duties in countries whose conditions are similar to those of Ireland as described by Mr. Pitt :—

"The only case in which, on mere principles of

* "Parliamentary Register," xvii., pp. 255, 256.

political economy, protecting duties can be defensible, is when they are imposed temporarily (especially in a young and rising nation) in the hopes of naturalising a foreign industry in itself perfectly suitable to the circumstances of the country. The superiority of one country over another in a branch of production often ⤪ arises only from having begun it sooner. There may be no inherent advantage on one part or disadvantage on the other, but only a present superiority of acquired skill and experience. A country which has this skill and experience yet to acquire may in other respects be better adapted to the production than those that were earlier in the field ; and, besides, it is a just remark of Mr. Rae that nothing has a greater tendency to promote improvements in any branch of production than its trial under a new set of conditions. But it cannot be expected that individuals should at their own risk, or rather to their certain loss, introduce a new manufacture and bear the burthen of carrying it on until the producers have been educated up to the level of those with whom the processes are traditional. A protecting duty continued for a reasonable time will sometimes be the least inconvenient mode in which the nation can tax itself for the support of such an experiment. But the protection should be confined to cases in which there is good ground of assurance that the industry which it fosters will, after a time, be able to dispense with it, nor should the domestic producers ever be allowed to expect that it will be continued to them beyond the time necessary for a fair trial of what they are capable of accomplishing."*

The Irish manufactures, which had revived by the protecting care of the Irish Parliament, died when that safeguard was removed.

Mr. Bushe, who was eighteen years Solicitor-General under a Tory Administration, and twenty years Chief Justice of Ireland, thus briefly described in the Irish Parliament the course of policy pursued by England towards the " sister country ":—

" For centuries have the British nation and Parliament kept you down, shackled your commerce, paralysed your exertions, despised your character, and ridiculed your pretensions to any privileges, commercial or constitutional."†

" I cannot think," says Mr. Chaplin, from his place in the English House of Commons, " that any reforms or remedial legislation that may be adopted (for Ireland) can be considered satisfactory or complete which do not include encouragement and, if necessary, assistance for the re-establishment of those industries which in former days were destroyed by the bitterly unjust and selfish policy of England."‡

* " Principles of Political Economy," p. 556.
† " Life of Plunket," ii., p. 354.
‡ Hansard, 261, Third Series, p. 836.

PRINTED BY CASSELL & COMPANY, LIMITED, LA BELLE SAUVAGE, LONDON, E.C.

Eleventh and Cheap Edition, cloth, **3s. 6d.**

The Life of the
Right Hon. W. E. Gladstone.

By G. BARNETT SMITH.

"A trustworthy and interesting picture of a noble life and character."—*Daily News*.

"A sober, solid, but interesting contribution to the political history of the Victorian epoch."—*Daily Telegraph*.

"The book should be read by every one who takes the least interest in the political history of the country."—*Daily Chronicle*.

"An elaborate and ably-written biography of Mr. Gladstone as a statesman and a writer."—*Echo*.

"Mr. Barnett Smith's Life of Mr. Gladstone is *a work of national importance*, and it should be read and studied by all classes."—*Nottingham Daily Express*.

"Many a thoughtful working man will hasten to add this book to his little store of fondly-cherished volumes."—*North British Daily Mail*.

"A very complete account of Mr. Gladstone's relations to the history of the past forty years."—*Observer*.

"A noble biography of a noble man."—*Aberdeen Free Press*.

"The minute accuracy of the painstaking record is indeed wonderful, considering the vastness of the field over which the biographer has been obliged to travel. *The volumes are, in fact, a history of England during the past half-century*, as well as a biography of the individual whose name they bear."—*Freeman*.

"The most superficial glance at the book is enough to secure the impression of great power in many departments on the part of the subject of it, and of great penetration, care, deliberation, and tact on the part of the author."—*Nonconformist*.

"*The most comprehensive and satisfactory Life of Mr. Gladstone* which has yet been compiled and given to the public."—*Edinburgh Daily Review*.

CASSELL & COMPANY, Limited, *Ludgate Hill, London*

𝕴llustrated, 𝕱ine-𝕬rt, and other 𝖁olumes.

Art, The Magazine of. Yearly Volume. With 500 choice Engravings. **16s.**

After London ; or, Wild England. By RICHARD JEFFERIES. **10s. 6d.**

Bismarck, Prince. By CHARLES LOWE, M.A. Two Vols., demy 8vo. With two Portraits. **24s.**

Bright, John, Life and Times of. By W. ROBERTSON. **7s. 6d.**

British Ballads. With 275 Original Illustrations. Two Vols. Cloth, **7s. 6d.** each.

British Battles on Land and Sea. By JAMES GRANT. With about 600 Illustrations. Three Vols., 4to, £1 7s. ; Library Edition, £1 10s.

British Battles, Recent. Illustrated. 4to, 9s. ; Library Edition, 10s.

Butterflies and Moths, European. By W. F. KIRBY. With 61 Coloured Plates. Demy 4to, 35s.

Canaries and Cage-Birds, The Illustrated Book of. By W. A. BLAKSTON, W. SWAYSLAND, and A. F. WIENER. With 56 Fac-simile Coloured Plates, 35s. Half-morocco, £2 5s.

Cassell's Family Magazine. Yearly Vol. Illustrated. 9s.

Cathedral Churches of England and Wales. With 150 Illustrations. 21s. *Édition de luxe,* £2 2s.

Changing Year, The. With Illustrations. 7s. 6d.

Choice Dishes at Small Cost. By A. G. PAYNE. 3s. 6d.

Choice Poems by H. W. Longfellow. Illustrated. 6s.

Cities of the World: their Origin, Progress, and Present Aspect. Three Vols. Illustrated. 7s. 6d. each.

Clinical Manuals for Practitioners and Students of Medicine. A List of Volumes forwarded post free on application to the Publishers.

Colonies and India, Our, How we Got Them, and Why we Keep Them. By Prof. C. RANSOME. 1s.

Columbus, Christopher, The Life and Voyages of. By WASHINGTON IRVING. Three Vols. 7s. 6d.

Cookery, Cassell's Dictionary of. Containing about Nine Thousand Recipes, 7s. 6d. ; Roxburgh, 10s. 6d.

Co-operators, Working Men: What they have Done, and What they are Doing. By A. H. DYKE-ACLAND, M.P., and B. JONES. 1s.

Cookery, A Year's. By PHYLLIS BROWNE. Cloth gilt, or oiled cloth, 3s. 6d.

Countries of the World, The. By ROBERT BROWN, M.A., Ph.D., &c. Complete in Six Vols., with about 750 Illustrations. 4to, 7s. 6d. each.

Cromwell, Oliver: The Man and his Mission. By J. ALLANSON PICTON, M.P. Cloth, 7s. 6d. ; morocco, cloth sides, 9s.

Cyclopædia, Cassell's Concise. With 12,000 subjects, brought down to the latest date. With about 600 Illustrations, 15s. ; Roxburgh, 18s.

Dairy Farming. By Prof. J. P. SHELDON. With 25 Fac-simile Coloured Plates, and numerous Wood Engravings. Cloth, 31s. 6d. ; half-morocco, 42s.

Decisive Events in History. By THOMAS ARCHER. With Sixteen Illustrations. Boards, 3s. 6d. ; cloth, 5s.

Decorative Design, Principles of. By CHRISTOPHER DRESSER, Ph.D. Illustrated. 5s.

Deserted Village Series, The. Consisting of *Éditions de luxe* of the most favourite poems of Standard Authors. Illustrated. 2s. 6d. each.

) GOLDSMITH'S DESERTED VILLAGE. | WORDSWORTH'S ODE ON IMMOR-
MILTON'S L'ALLEGRO AND IL | TALITY, AND LINES ON TIN-
PENSEROSO. | TERN ABBEY.

Dickens, Character Sketches from. SECOND and THIRD SERIES. With Six Original Drawings in each, by FREDERICK BARNARD. In Portfolio. 21s. each.

Diary of Two Parliaments. The Disraeli Parliament. By H. W. LUCY. 12s.

Dog, The By IDSTONE. Illustrated. 2s. 6d.

Dog, Illustrated Book of the. By VERO SHAW, B.A. With 28 Coloured Plates. Cloth bevelled, 35s. ; half-morocco, 45s.

Domestic Dictionary, The. An Encyclopædia for the Household. Cloth, 7s. 6d.

Doré's Adventures of Munchausen. Illustrated by GUSTAVE DORÉ. 5s.

Doré's Dante's Inferno. Illustrated by GUSTAVE DORÉ. *Popular Edition*, 21s.

Doré's Don Quixote. With about 400 Illustrations by DORÉ. 15s.

Doré's Fairy Tales Told Again. With 24 Full-page Engravings by GUSTAVE DORÉ. 5s.

Doré Gallery, The. *Popular Edition* With 250 Illustrations by GUSTAVE DORÉ. 4to, 42s.

Doré's Milton's Paradise Lost. With Full-page Drawings by GUSTAVE DORÉ. 4to, 21s.

Edinburgh, Old and New, Cassell's. Three Vols. With 600 Illustrations. 9s. each.

Educational Year-Book, The. 6s.

Egypt : Descriptive, Historical, and Picturesque. By Prof. G. EBERS. Translated by CLARA BELL, with Notes by SAMUEL BIRCH, LL.D., &c. Two Vols. With 800 Original Engravings. Vol. I., £2 5s. ; Vol. II., £2 12s. 6d. Complete in box, £4 17s. 6d.

Electrician's Pocket-Book, The. By GORDON WIGAN, M.A. 5s.

Encyclopædic Dictionary, The. A New and Original Work of Reference to all the Words in the English Language. Nine Divisional Vols. now ready, 10s. 6d. each ; or the Double Divisional Vols., half-
· morocco, 21s. each.

Energy in Nature. By WM. LANT CARPENTER, B.A., B.Sc. 80 Illustrations. 3s. 6d.

England, Cassell's Illustrated History of. With 2,000 Illustrations. Ten Vols., 4to, 9s. each.

English History, The Dictionary of. Cloth, 21s. ; Roxburgh, 25s.

English Literature, Library of. By Prof. HENRY MORLEY.

VOL. I.—SHORTER ENGLISH POEMS, 12s. 6d.
VOL. II.—ILLUSTRATIONS OF ENGLISH RELIGION, 11s. 6d.
VOL. III.—ENGLISH PLAYS, 11s. 6d.
VOL. IV.—SHORTER WORKS IN ENGLISH PROSE, 11s. 6d.
VOL. V.—SKETCHES OF LONGER WORKS IN ENGLISH VERSE
AND PROSE, 11s. 6d.

Five Volumes handsomely bound in half-morocco, £5 5s.

Volumes I., II., and III. of the Popular Edition are now ready, price 7s. 6d. each.

English Literature, The Story of. By ANNA BUCKLAND. 5s.

English Literature, Dictionary of. By W. DAVENPORT ADAMS. *Cheap Edition*, 7s. 6d.; Roxburgh, 10s. 6d.

English Poetesses. By ERIC S. ROBERTSON, M.A. 5s.

Æsop's Fables. With about 150 Illustrations by E. GRISET. Cloth, 7s. 6d.; gilt edges, 10s. 6d.

Etiquette of Good Society. 1s. ; cloth, 1s. 6d.

Family Physician, The. By Eminent PHYSICIANS and SURGEONS. Cloth, 21s. ; half-morocco, 25s.

Far, Far West, Life and Labour in the. By W. HENRY BARNEBY. With Map of Route. Cloth, 16s.

Fenn, G. Manville, Works by. *Popular Editions.* Cloth boards, 2s. each.

SWEET MACE.	THE VICAR'S PEOPLE.
DUTCH, THE DIVER ; OR, A MAN'S MISTAKE.	COBWEB'S FATHER, AND OTHER STORIES.
MY PATIENTS. Being the Notes of a Navy Surgeon.	THE PARSON O' DUMFORD.
	POVERTY CORNER.

Ferns, European. By JAMES BRITTEN, F.L.S. With 30 Fac-simile Coloured Plates by D. BLAIR, F.L.S. 21s.

Field Naturalist's Handbook, The. By the Rev. J. G. WOOD and THEODORE WOOD. 5s.

Figuier's Popular Scientific Works. With Several Hundred Illustrations in each. 3s. 6d. each.

THE HUMAN RACE.	THE OCEAN WORLD.
WORLD BEFORE THE DELUGE.	THE VEGETABLE WORLD.
REPTILES AND BIRDS.	THE INSECT WORLD.

MAMMALIA.

Fine-Art Library, The. Edited by JOHN SPARKES, Principal of the South Kensington Art Schools. Each Book contains about 100 Illustrations. 5s. each.

TAPESTRY. By Eugene Müntz. Translated by Miss L. J. Davis.	GREEK ARCHÆOLOGY. By Maxime Collignon. Translated by Dr. J. H. Wright, Associate Professor of Greek in Dartmouth Coll., U.S.A.
ENGRAVING. By Le Vicomte Henri Delaborde. Translated by R. A. M. Stevenson.	
THE ENGLISH SCHOOL OF PAINTING. By E. Chesneau. Translated by L. N. Etherington. With an Introduction by Prof. Ruskin.	ARTISTIC ANATOMY. By Prof. Duval. Translated by F. E. Fenton.
THE FLEMISH SCHOOL OF PAINTING. By A. J. Wauters. Translated by Mrs. Henry Rossel.	THE DUTCH SCHOOL OF PAINTING. By Henry Havard. Translated by G. Powell.

Fisheries of the World, The. Illustrated. 4to. 9s.

Five Pound Note, The, and other Stories. By G. S. JEALOUS. 1s.

Forging of the Anchor, The. A Poem. By Sir SAMUEL FERGUSON, LL.D. With 20 Original Illustrations. Gilt edges, 5s.

Fossil Reptiles, A History of British. By Sir RICHARD OWEN, K.C.B., F.R.S., &c. With 268 Plates. In Four Vols., £12 12s.

Four Years of Irish History (1845-49). By Sir GAVAN DUFFY, K.C.M.G. 21s.

Franco-German War, Cassell's History of the. Two Vols. With 500 Illustrations. 9s. each.

Garden Flowers, Familiar. FIRST, SECOND, THIRD, and FOURTH
SERIES. By SHIRLEY HIBBERD. With Original Paintings by F. E.
HULME, F.R.S. With 40 Full-page Coloured Plates in each Cloth
gilt, in cardboard box (or in morocco, cloth sides), 12s. 6d. each.

Gardening, Cassell's Popular. Illustrated. Vols. I., II., and III.,
5s. each.

Gladstone, Life of W. E. By BARNETT SMITH. With Portrait, 3s. 6d.
Jubilee Edition, 1s.

Gleanings from Popular Authors. Two Vols. With Original Illustrations. 4to, 9s. each. Two Vols. in One, 15s.

Great Industries of Great Britain. Three Vols. With about 400
Illustrations. 4to., cloth, 7s. 6d. each.

Great Painters of Christendom, The, from Cimabue to Wilkie.
By JOHN FORBES-ROBERTSON. Illustrated throughout. 12s. 6d.

Great Western Railway, The Official Illustrated Guide to the.
With Illustrations, 1s. ; cloth, 2s.

Gulliver's Travels. With 88 Engravings by MORTEN. *Cheap Edition*, 5s.

Guide to Employment in the Civil Service. 3s. 6d.

Guide to Female Employment in Government Offices. 1s.

Gun and its Development, The. By W. W. GREENER. With 500
Illustrations. 10s. 6d.

Health, The Book of. By Eminent Physicians and Surgeons. Cloth,
21s. ; half-morocco, 25s.

Heavens, The Story of the. By ROBERT STAWELL BALL, LL.D.,
F.R.S., F.R.A.S., Royal Astronomer of Ireland. With 16 *Separate
Plates* printed by Chromo-Lithography, and 90 Wood Engravings.
Demy 8vo, 544 pages, cloth. 31s. 6d.

Heroes of Britain in Peace and War. In Two Vols., with 300
Original Illustrations. Cloth, 5s. each.

Horse, The Book of the. By SAMUEL SIDNEY. With 25 *fac-simile*
Coloured Plates. Demy 4to, 31s. 6d. ; half-morocco, £2 2s.

Horses, The Simple Ailments of. By W. F. Illustrated. 5s.

Household Guide, Cassell's. With Illustrations and Coloured Plates.
Two Double Vols., half-calf, 31s. 6d.; Library Edition, Two Vols., 24s.

How Women may Earn a Living. By MERCY GROGAN. 1s.

India, The Coming Struggle for. By Prof. ARMINIUS VAMBÉRY.
With Map in Colours. 5s.

India, Cassell's History of. By JAMES GRANT. With about 400
Illustrations. Two Vols., 9s. each.

India : the Land and the People. By Sir JAMES CAIRD, K.C.B.
10s. 6d.

**In-door Amusements, Card Games, and Fireside Fun, Cassell's
Book of.** Illustrated. 3s. 6d.

International Portrait Gallery, The. Two Vols., each containing 20
Portraits in Colours. 12s. 6d. each.

Invisible Life, Vignettes from. By JOHN BADCOCK, F.R.M.S.
Illustrated. 3s. 6d.

Irish Parliament, The ; What it Was and What it Did. By J. G.
SWIFT MCNEILL, M.A. 1s.

Italy. By. J. W. PROBYN. 7s. 6d.

Kennel Guide, Practical. By Dr. GORDON STABLES. Illustrated. 2s. 6d.

Khiva, A Ride to. By the late Col. FRED BURNABY. 1s. 6d.

Ladies' Physician, The. By a London Physician. 6s.

Land Question, The. By. Prof. J. ELLIOT, M.R.A.C. 10s. 6d.

Landscape Painting in Oils, A Course of Lessons in. By A. F. GRACE. With Nine Reproductions in Colour. *Cheap Edition*, 25s.

Law, About Going to. By A. J. WILLIAMS. 2s. 6d.

London & North-Western Railway Official Illustrated Guide. 1s. ; cloth, 2s.

London, Greater. By EDWARD WALFORD. Two Vols. With about 400 Illustrations. 9s. each.

London, Old and New. Six Vols., each containing about 200 Illustrations and Maps. Cloth, 9s. each.

London's Roll of Fame. With Portraits and Illustrations. 12s. 6d.

Longfellow's Poetical Works. Illustrated. £3 3s.

Love's Extremes, At. By MAURICE THOMPSON. 5s.

Mechanics, The Practical Dictionary of. Containing 15,000 Drawings. Four Vols. 21s. each.

Medicine, Manuals for Students of. (*A List forwarded post free on application.*)

Microscope, The ; and some of the Wonders it Reveals. 1s.

Midland Railway, Official Illustrated Guide to the. 1s. ; cloth, 2s.

Modern Artists, Some. With highly-finished Engravings. 12s. 6d.

Modern Europe, A History of. By C. A. FYFFE, M.A. Vol. I. from 1792 to 1814. 12s.

National Portrait Gallery, The. Each Volume containing 20 Portraits, printed in Chromo-Lithography. Four Vols., 12s. 6d. each ; or in Two Double Vols., 21s. each.

Natural History, Cassell's Concise. By E. PERCEVAL WRIGHT, M.A., M.D., F.L.S. With several Hundred Illustrations. 7s. 6d.

Natural History, Cassell's New. Edited by Prof. P. MARTIN DUNCAN. M.B., F.R.S., F.G.S. With Contributions by Eminent Scientific Writers. Complete in Six Vols. With about 2,000 high-class Illustrations. Extra crown 4to, cloth, 9s. each.

Natural History, Cassell's Popular. With about 2,000 Engravings and Coloured Plates. Complete in Four Vols. Cloth gilt, 42s.

Nature, Short Studies from. Illustrated. 5s.

Nursing for the Home and for the Hospital, A Handbook of. By CATHERINE J. WOOD. *Cheap Edition.* 1s. 6d. ; cloth, 2s.

On the Equator. By H. DE W. Illustrated with Photos. 3s. 6d.

Our Homes, and How to Make them Healthy. By Eminent Authorities. Illustrated. 15s. ; half-morocco, 21s.

Our Own Country. Six Vols. With 1,200 Illustrations. Cloth, 7s. 6d. each.

Outdoor Sports and Indoor Amusements. With nearly 1,000 Illustrations. 9s.

Paris, Cassell's Illustrated Guide to. 1s. ; cloth, 2s.

Parliaments, A Diary of Two. By H. W. LUCY. The Disraeli Parliament, 1874—1880. 12s.

Paxton's Flower Garden. By Sir JOSEPH PAXTON and Prof. LINDLEY. Revised by THOMAS BAINES, F.R.H.S. Three Vols. With 100 Coloured Plates. £1 1s. each.

Peoples of the World, The. Vols. I. to V. By Dr. ROBERT BROWN. With Illustrations. 7s. 6d. each.

Perak and the Malays. By Major FRED McNAIR. Illustrated. 10s. 6d.

Photography for Amateurs. By T. C. HEPWORTH. Illustrated. 1s.; or cloth, 1s. 6d.

Phrase and Fable, Dictionary of. By the Rev. Dr. BREWER. *Cheap Edition, Enlarged*, cloth, 3s. 6d. ; or with leather back, 4s. 6d.

Pictures from English Literature. With Full-page Illustrations. 5s.

Pictures of Bird Life in Pen and Pencil. Illustrated. 21s.

Picturesque America. Complete in Four Vols., with 48 Exquisite Steel Plates and about 800 Original Wood Engravings. £2 2s. each.

Picturesque Canada. With about 600 Original Illustrations. Two Vols. £3 3s. each.

Picturesque Europe. Complete in Five Vols. Each containing 13 Exquisite Steel Plates, from Original Drawings, and nearly 200 Original Illustrations. £10 10s.; half-morocco, £15 15s.; morocco gilt, £26 5s. The POPULAR EDITION is published in Five Vols., 18s. each, of which Four Vols. are now ready.

Pigeon Keeper, The Practical. By LEWIS WRIGHT. Illustrated. 3s. 6d.

Pigeons, The Book of. By ROBERT FULTON. Edited and Arranged by LEWIS WRIGHT. With 50 Coloured Plates and numerous Wood Engravings. 31s. 6d. ; half-morocco, £2 2s.

Poems and Pictures. With numerous Illustrations. 5s.

Poets, Cassell's Miniature Library of the :—

BURNS. Two Vols. 2s. 6d.	MILTON. Two Vols. 2s. 6d.
BYRON. Two Vols. 2s. 6d.	SCOTT. Two Vols. 2s. 6d. [2s. 6d.
HOOD. Two Vols. 2s. 6d.	SHERIDAN and GOLDSMITH. 2 Vols.
LONGFELLOW. Two Vols. 2s. 6d.	WORDSWORTH. Two Vols. 2s. 6d.

SHAKESPEARE. Twelve Vols., in Case, 15s.

Police Code, and Manual of the Criminal Law. By C. E. HOWARD VINCENT, M.P. 2s.

Popular Library, Cassell's. A Series of New and Original Works. Cloth, 1s. each.

THE RUSSIAN EMPIRE.	DOMESTIC FOLK LORE.
THE RELIGIOUS REVOLUTION IN THE 16TH CENTURY.	THE REV. ROWLAND HILL: Preacher and Wit.
ENGLISH JOURNALISM.	BOSWELL AND JOHNSON : their Companions and Contemporaries.
THE HUGUENOTS.	
OUR COLONIAL EMPIRE.	
JOHN WESLEY.	THE SCOTTISH COVENANTERS.
THE YOUNG MAN IN THE BATTLE OF LIFE.	HISTORY OF THE FREE-TRADE MOVEMENT IN ENGLAND.
THE STORY OF THE ENGLISH JACOBINS.	

Poultry Keeper, The Practical. By L. WRIGHT. With Coloured Plates and Illustrations. 3s. 6d.

Poultry, The Illustrated Book of. By L. WRIGHT. With Fifty Exquisite Coloured Plates, and numerous Wood Engravings. Cloth, 31s. 6d. ; half-morocco, £2 2s.

Poultry, The Book of. By LEWIS WRIGHT. *Popular Edition.* With Illustrations on Wood, 10s. 6d.

Quiver Yearly Volume, The. With about 300 Original Contributions by Eminent Divines and Popular Authors, and upwards of 250 high-class Illustrations. 7s. 6d.

Rabbit-Keeper, The Practical. By CUNICULUS. Illustrated. 3s. 6d

Rainbow Series, Cassell's, of New and Original Novels. Price 1s. each.

As it was Written. By S. Luska.	A Crimson Stain. By A Bradshaw.
Morgan's Horror. By G. Manville Fenn.	

Rays from the Realms of Nature. By the Rev. J. Neil, M.A. Illustrated. 2s. 6d.

Red Library of English and American Classics, The. Stiff covers, 1s. each; cloth, 2s. each; or half-calf, marbled edges, 5s.

Washington Irving's Sketch Book.	American Humour.
The Last Days of Palmyra.	Sketches by Boz.
Tales of the Borders.	Macaulay's Lays, and Selected Essays.
Pride and Prejudice.	Harry Lorrequer.
The Last of the Mohicans.	The Old Curiosity Shop.
The Heart of Midlothian.	Rienzi.
The Last Days of Pompeii.	The Talisman.

Romeo and Juliet. *Édition de Luxe.* Illustrated with Twelve Superb Photogravures from Original Drawings by F. Dicksee, A.R.A. £5 5s.

Royal River, The: The Thames from Source to Sea. With Descriptive Text and a Series of beautiful Engravings. £2 2s.

Russia. By D. Mackenzie Wallace, M.A. 5s.

Russo-Turkish War, Cassell's History of. With about 500 Illustrations. Two Vols., 9s. each.

Sandwith, Humphry. A Memoir by his Nephew, Thomas Humphry Ward. 7s. 6d.

Saturday Journal, Cassell's. Yearly Volume. 6s.

Science for All. Edited by Dr. Robert Brown, M.A., F.L.S., &c. With 1,500 Illustrations. Five Vols. 9s. each.

Sea, The: Its Stirring Story of Adventure, Peril, and Heroism. By F. Whymper. With 400 Illustrations. Four Vols., 7s. 6d. each.

Shakspere, The Leopold. With 400 Illustrations. Cloth, 6s.

Shakspere, The Royal. With Steel Plates and Wood Engravings. Three Vols. 15s. each.

Shakespeare, Cassell's Quarto Edition. Edited by Charles and Mary Cowden Clarke, and containing about 600 Illustrations by H. C. Selous. Complete in Three Vols., cloth gilt, £3 3s.

Sketching from Nature in Water Colours. By Aaron Penley. With Illustrations in Chromo-Lithography. 15s.

Smith, The Adventures and Discourses of Captain John. By John Ashton. Illustrated. 5s.

Sports and Pastimes, Cassell's Book of. With more than 800 Illustrations and Coloured Frontispiece. 768 pages. 7s. 6d.

Steam Engine, The Theory and Action of the: for Practical Men. By W. H. Northcott, C.E. 3s. 6d.

Stock Exchange Year-Book, The. By Thomas Skinner. 10s. 6d.

Stones of London, The. By E. F. Flower. 6d.

"Stories from Cassell's." 6d. each; cloth lettered, 9d. each.

My Aunt's Match-making.	"Running Pilot."
Told by her Sister.	The Mortgage Money.
The Silver Lock.	Gourlay Brothers.

A Great Mistake.

*** The above are also issued, Three Volumes in One, cloth, price 2s. each.

Sunlight and Shade. With numerous Exquisite Engravings. 7s. 6d.

Telegraph Guide, The. Illustrated. 1s.

Trajan. An American Novel. By H. F. Keenan. 7s. 6d.

Transformations of Insects, The. By Prof. P. MARTIN DUNCAN, M.B., F.R.S. With 240 Illustrations. 6s.

Treatment, The Year-Book of. A Critical Review for Practitioners of Medicine and Surgery. 5s.

"Unicode": the Universal Telegraph Phrase Book. 2s. 6d.

United States, Cassell's History of the. By EDMUND OLLIER. With 600 Illustrations. Three Vols. 9s. each.

United States, Constitutional History and Political Development of the. By SIMON STERNE, of the New York Bar. 5s.

Universal History, Cassell's Illustrated. Four Vols. 9s. each.

Vicar of Wakefield and other Works by OLIVER GOLDSMITH. Illustrated. 3s. 6d.

Wealth Creation. By A. MONGREDIEN. 5s.

Westall, W., Novels by. *Popular Editions.* Cloth, 2s. each.
RALPH NORBRECK'S TRUST.
THE OLD FACTORY. RED RYVINGTON.

What Girls Can Do. By PHYLLIS BROWNE. 2s. 6d.

Wild Animals and Birds: their Haunts and Habits. By Dr. ANDREW WILSON. Illustrated. 7s. 6d.

Wild Birds, Familiar. First and Second Series. By W. SWAYSLAND. With 40 Coloured Plates in each. 12s. 6d. each.

Wild Flowers, Familiar. By F. E. HULME, F.L.S.. F.S.A. Five Series. With 40 Coloured Plates in each. 12s. 6d. each.

Winter in India, A. By the Rt. Hon. W. E. BAXTER, M.P. 5s.

Wise Woman, The. By GEORGE MACDONALD. 2s. 6d.

Wood Magic: A Fable. By RICHARD JEFFERIES. 6s.

World of the Sea. Translated from the French of MOQUIN TANDON, by the Very Rev. H. MARTYN HART, M.A. Illustrated. Cloth. 6s.

World of Wit and Humour, The. With 400 Illustrations. Cloth, 7s. 6d.; cloth gilt, gilt edges, 10s. 6d.

World of Wonders. Two Vols. With 400 Illustrations. 7s. 6d. each.

MAGAZINES.

The Quiver, for Sunday Reading. Monthly, 6d.

Cassell's Family Magazine. Monthly, 7d.

"Little Folks" Magazine. Monthly, 6d.

The Magazine of Art. Monthly, 1s.

Cassell's Saturday Journal. Weekly, 1d.; Monthly, 6d.

*** *Full particulars of CASSELL & COMPANY'S Monthly Serial Publications, numbering upwards of 50 different Works, will be found in* CASSELL & COMPANY'S COMPLETE CATALOGUE, *sent post free on application.*

Catalogues of CASSELL & COMPANY'S PUBLICATIONS, which may be had at all Booksellers', or will be sent post free on application to the publishers:—

CASSELL'S COMPLETE CATALOGUE, containing particulars of One Thousand Volumes.

CASSELL'S CLASSIFIED CATALOGUE, in which their Works are arranged according to price, from *Sixpence to Twenty-five Guineas.*

CASSELL'S EDUCATIONAL CATALOGUE, containing particulars of CASSELL & COMPANY'S Educational Works and Students' Manuals.

CASSELL & COMPANY, LIMITED, *Ludgate Hill, London.*

Bibles and Religious Works.

Bible, The Crown Illustrated. With about 1,000 Original Illustrations. With References, &c. 1,248 pages, crown 4to, cloth, 7s. 6d.

Bible, Cassell's Illustrated Family. With 900 Illustrations. Leather, gilt edges, £2 10s.

Bible Dictionary, Cassell's. With nearly 600 Illustrations. 7s. 6d.

Bible Educator, The. Edited by the Very Rev. Dean PLUMPTRE, D.D., Wells. With Illustrations, Maps, &c. Four Vols., cloth, 6s. each.

Bunyan's Pilgrim's Progress (Cassell's Illustrated). Demy 4to. Illustrated throughout. 7s. 6d.

Bunyan's Pilgrim's Progress. With Illustrations. Cloth, 3s. 6d.

Child's Life of Christ, The. Complete in One Handsome Volume, with about 200 Original Illustrations. Demy 4to, gilt edges, 21s.

Child's Bible, The. With 200 Illustrations. Demy 4to, 830 pp. 143*rd Thousand. Cheap Edition,* 7s. 6d.

Church at Home, The. A Series of Short Sermons. By the Rt. Rev. ROWLEY HILL, D.D., Bishop of Sodor and Man. 5s.

Day-Dawn in Dark Places; or Wanderings and Work in Bechwanaland, South Africa. By the Rev. JOHN MACKENZIE. Illustrated throughout. Cloth, 3s. 6d.

Difficulties of Belief, Some. By the Rev. T. TEIGNMOUTH SHORE, M.A. *New and Cheap Edition.* 2s. 6d.

Doré Bible. With 230 Illustrations by GUSTAVE DORÉ. Cloth, £2 10s.; Persian morocco, £3 10s.

Early Days of Christianity, The. By the Ven. Archdeacon FARRAR, D.D., F.R.S.
    LIBRARY EDITION. Two Vols., 24s.; morocco, £2 2s.
    POPULAR EDITION. Complete in One Volume, cloth, 6s.; cloth, gilt edges, 7s. 6d.; Persian morocco, 10s. 6d.; tree-calf, 15s.

Family Prayer-Book, The. Edited by Rev. Canon GARBETT, M.A., and Rev. S. MARTIN. Extra crown 4to, cloth, 5s.; morocco, 18s.

Geikie, Cunningham, D.D., Works by :—
    HOURS WITH THE BIBLE. Six Vols., 6s. each.
    ENTERING ON LIFE. 3s. 6d.
    THE PRECIOUS PROMISES. 2s. 6d.
    THE ENGLISH REFORMATION. 5s.
    OLD TESTAMENT CHARACTERS. 6s.
    THE LIFE AND WORDS OF CHRIST. Two Vols., cloth, 30s. *Students' Edition.* Two Vols., 16s.

Glories of the Man of Sorrows, The. Sermons preached at St. James's, Piccadilly. By the Rev. H. G. BONAVIA HUNT. 2s. 6d.

Gospel of Grace, The. By A. LINDESIE. Cloth, 3s. 6d.

"Heart Chords." A Series of Works by Eminent Divines. Bound in cloth, red edges, One Shilling each.

MY FATHER.
MY BIBLE.
MY WORK FOR GOD.
MY OBJECT IN LIFE.
MY ASPIRATIONS.
MY EMOTIONAL LIFE.
MY BODY.

MY SOUL.
MY GROWTH IN DIVINE LIFE.
MY HEREAFTER.
MY WALK WITH GOD.
MY AIDS TO THE DIVINE LIFE.
MY SOURCES OF STRENGTH.

Life of Christ, The. By the Ven. Archdeacon FARRAR, D.D., F.R.S., Chaplain-in-Ordinary to the Queen.
> ILLUSTRATED EDITION, with about 300 Original Illustrations. Extra crown 4to, cloth, gilt edges, 21s. ; morocco antique, 42s.
> LIBRARY EDITION. Two Vols. Cloth, 24s. ; morocco, 42s.
> BIJOU EDITION. Five Volumes, in box, 10s. 6d. the set.
> POPULAR EDITION, in One Vol. 8vo, cloth, 6s. ; cloth, gilt edges, 7s. 6d. ; Persian morocco, gilt edges, 10s. 6d. ; tree-calf, 15s.

Marriage Ring, The. By WILLIAM LANDELS, D.D. Bound in white leatherette, gilt edges, in box, 6s. ; morocco, 8s. 6d.

Martyrs, Foxe's Book of. With about 200 Illustrations. Imperial 8vo, 732 pages, cloth, 12s. ; cloth gilt, gilt edges, 15s.

Moses and Geology ; or, The Harmony of the Bible with Science. By SAMUEL KINNS, Ph.D., F.R.A.S. Illustrated. *Cheap Edition*, 6s.

Music of the Bible, The. By J. STAINER, M.A., Mus. Doc. 2s. 6d.

Near and the Heavenly Horizons, The. By the Countess DE GASPARIN. 1s. ; cloth, 2s.

New Testament Commentary for English Readers, The. Edited by the Rt. Rev. C. J. ELLICOTT, D.D., Lord Bishop of Gloucester and Bristol. In Three Volumes, 21s. each.
> Vol. I.—The Four Gospels.
> Vol. II.—The Acts, Romans, Corinthians, Galatians.
> Vol. III.—The remaining Books of the New Testament.

Old Testament Commentary for English Readers, The. Edited by the Right Rev. C. J. ELLICOTT, D.D., Lord Bishop of Gloucester and Bristol. Complete in 5 Vols., 21s. each.

Vol. I.—Genesis to Numbers.	Vol. III.—Kings I. to Esther.
Vol. II.—Deuteronomy to Samuel II.	Vol. IV.—Job to Isaiah.
	Vol. V.—Jeremiah to Malachi.

Patriarchs, The. By the late Rev. W. HANNA, D.D., and the Ven. Archdeacon NORRIS, B.D. 2s. 6d.

Protestantism, The History of. By the Rev. J. A. WYLIE, LL.D. Containing upwards of 600 Original Illustrations. Three Vols., 27s.

Quiver Yearly Volume, The. 250 high-class Illustrations. 7s. 6d.

Revised Version—Commentary on the Revised Version of the New Testament. By the Rev. W. G. HUMPHRY, B.D. 7s. 6d.

Sacred Poems, The Book of. Edited by the Rev. Canon BAYNES, M.A. With Illustrations. Cloth, gilt edges, 5s.

St. George for England ; and other Sermons preached to Children. By the Rev. T. TEIGNMOUTH SHORE, M.A. 5s.

St. Paul, The Life and Work of. By the Ven. Archdeacon FARRAR, D.D., F.R.S., Chaplain in Ordinary to the Queen.
> LIBRARY EDITION. Two Vols., cloth, 24s. ; morocco, 42s.
> ILLUSTRATED EDITION, complete in One Volume, with about 300 Illustrations, £1 1s. ; morocco, £2 2s.
> POPULAR EDITION. One Volume, 8vo, cloth, 6s. ; cloth, gilt edges, 7s. 6d. ; Persian morocco, 10s. 6d. ; tree-calf, 15s.

Secular Life, The Gospel of the. Sermons preached at Oxford. By the Hon. W. H. FREMANTLE, Canon of Canterbury. 5s.

Sermons Preached at Westminster Abbey. By ALFRED BARRY, D.D., D.C.L., Primate of Australia. 5s.

Shall We Know One Another ? By the Rt. Rev. J. C. RYLE, D.D., Bishop of Liverpool. *New and Enlarged Edition.* Cloth limp, 1s.

Simon Peter: His Life, Times, and Friends. By E. HODDER. 5s.

Voice of Time, The. By JOHN STROUD. Cloth gilt, 1s.

Educational Works and Students' Manuals.

Algebra, The Elements of. By Prof. WALLACE, M.A., 1s.

Arithmetics, The Modern School. By GEORGE RICKS, B.Sc. Lond. With Test Cards. (*List on application.*)

Book-Keeping:—
Book-Keeping for Schools. By Theodore Jones, 2s. ; cloth, 3s.
Book-Keeping for the Million. By T. Jones, 2s. ; cloth, 3s.
Books for Jones's System. Ruled Sets of, 2s.

Commentary, The New Testament. Edited by the Lord Bishop of GLOUCESTER and BRISTOL. Handy Volume Edition.
St. Matthew, 3s. 6d. St. Mark, 3s. St. Luke, 3s. 6d. St. John, 3s. 6d. The Acts of the Apostles, 3s. 6d. Romans, 2s. 6d. Corinthians I. and II., 3s. Galatians, Ephesians, and Philippians, 3s. Colossians, Thessalonians, and Timothy, 3s. Titus, Philemon, Hebrews, and James, 3s. Peter, Jude, and John, 3s. The Revelation, 3s. An Introduction to the New Testament, 3s. 6d.

Commentary, Old Testament. Edited by Bishop ELLICOTT. Handy Volume Edition. In Vols. suitable for School and general use. Genesis, 3s. 6d. Exodus, 3s. Leviticus, 3s. Numbers, 2s. 6d. Deuteronomy, 2s. 6d.

Copy-Books, Cassell's Graduated. *Eighteen Books.* 2d. each.

Copy-Books, The Modern School. In Twelve Books, of 24 pages each, price 2d. each.

Drawing Books for Young Artists. 4 Books. 6d. each.

Drawing Books, Superior. 3 Books. Printed in Fac-simile by Lithography, price 5s. each.

Drawing Copies, Cassell's Modern School Freehand. First Grade, 1s. ; Second Grade, 2s.

Energy and Motion: A Text-Book of Elementary Mechanics. By WILLIAM PAICE, M.A. Illustrated. 1s. 6d.

English Literature, A First Sketch of, from the Earliest Period to the Present Time. By Prof. HENRY MORLEY. 7s. 6d.

Euclid, Cassell's. Edited by Prof. WALLACE, A.M. 1s.

Euclid, The First Four Books of. In paper, 6d. ; cloth, 9d.

French, Cassell's Lessons in. *New and Revised Edition.* Parts I. and II., each 2s. 6d. ; complete, 4s. 6d. Key, 1s. 6d.

French-English and English-French Dictionary. *Entirely New and Enlarged Edition.* 1,150 pages, 8vo, cloth, 3s. 6d.

Galbraith and Haughton's Scientific Manuals. By the Rev. Prof. GALBRAITH, M.A., and the Rev. Prof. HAUGHTON, M.D., D.C.L. Arithmetic, 3s. 6d.—Plane Trigonometry, 2s. 6d.—Euclid, Books I., II., III., 2s. 6d.—Books IV., V., VI. 2s. 6d.—Mathematical Tables, 3s. 6d.—Mechanics, 3s. 6d.—Optics, 2s. 6d.—Hydrostatics, 3s. 6d.— Astronomy, 5s.—Steam Engine, 3s. 6d.—Algebra, Part I., cloth, 2s. 6d. ; Complete, 7s. 6d.—Tides and Tidal Currents, with Tidal Cards, 3s.

German-English and English-German Dictionary. 3s. 6d.

German Reading, First Lessons in. By A. JAGST. Illustrated. 1s.

Handbook of New Code of Regulations. By JOHN F. MOSS. 1s.

Historical Course for Schools, Cassell's. Illustrated throughout. I. Stories from English History, 1s. II.—The Simple Outline of English History, 1s. 3d. III.—The Class History of England, 2s. 6d.

Latin-English and English-Latin Dictionary. By J. R. BEARD, D.D., and C. BEARD, B.A. Crown 8vo, 914 pp., 3s. 6d.

Little Folks' History of England. By ISA CRAIG-KNOX. With 30 Illustrations. 1s. 6d.

Making of the Home, The: A Book of Domestic Economy for School and Home Use. By Mrs. SAMUEL A. BARNETT. 1s. 6d.

Marlborough Books:—Arithmetic Examples, 3s. Arithmetic Rules, 1s. 6d. French Exercises, 3s. 6d. French Grammar, 2s. 6d. German Grammar, 3s. 6d.

Music, An Elementary Manual of. By HENRY LESLIE. 1s.

Natural Philosophy. By Rev. Prof. HAUGHTON, F.R.S. Illustrated. 3s. 6d.

Painting, Guides to. With Coloured Plates and full instructions:—Animal Painting, 5s.—China Painting, 5s.—Figure Painting, 7s. 6d.—Flower Painting, 2 Books, 5s. each. — Tree Painting, 5s.—Sepia Painting, 5s.—Water Colour Painting, 5s.—Neutral Tint, 5s.

Popular Educator, Cassell's. *New and Thoroughly Revised Edition.* Illustrated throughout. Complete in Six Vols., 5s. each.

Physical Science, Intermediate Text-Book of. By F. H. BOWMAN, D.Sc. F.R.A.S., F.L.S. Illustrated. 3s. 6d.

Readers, Cassell's Readable. Carefully graduated, extremely interesting, and illustrated throughout. (*List on application.*)

Readers, Cassell's Historical. Illustrated throughout, printed on superior paper, and strongly bound in cloth. (*List on application.*)

Readers, The Modern Geographical, illustrated throughout, and strongly bound in cloth. (*List on application.*)

Readers, The Modern School. Illustrated. (*List on application.*)

Reading and Spelling Book, Cassell's Illustrated. 1s.

Right Lines; or, Form and Colour. With Illustrations. 1s.

School Manager's Manual. By F. C. MILLS, M.A. 1s.

Shakspere's Plays for School Use. 5 Books. Illustrated, 6d. each.

Shakspere Reading Book, The. By H. COURTHOPE BOWEN, M.A. Illustrated. 3s. 6d. Also issued in Three Books, 1s. each.

Spelling, A Complete Manual of. By J. D. MORELL, LL.D. 1s.

Technical Manuals, Cassell's. Illustrated throughout:—Handrailing and Staircasing, 3s. 6d.—Bricklayers, Drawing for, 3s.—Building Construction, 2s.—Cabinet-Makers, Drawing for, 3s.—Carpenters and Joiners, Drawing for, 3s. 6d.—Gothic Stonework, 3s.—Linear Drawing and Practical Geometry, 2s.—Linear Drawing and Projection. The Two Vols. in One, 3s. 6d.—Machinists and Engineers, Drawing for, 4s. 6d.—Metal-Plate Workers, Drawing for, 3s.—Model Drawing, 3s.—Orthographical and Isometrical Projection, 2s.—Practical Perspective, 3s.—Stonemasons, Drawing for, 3s.—Applied Mechanics, by Prof. R. S. Ball, LL.D., 2s.—Systematic Drawing and Shading, by Charles Ryan, 2s.

Technical Educator, Cassell's. Four Vols., 6s. each. Popular Edition, in Four Vols., 5s. each.

Technology, Manuals of. Edited by Prof. AYRTON, F.R.S., and RICHARD WORMELL, D.Sc., M.A. Illustrated throughout:—The Dyeing of Textile Fabrics, by Prof. Hummel, 5s.—Watch and Clock Making, by D. Glasgow, 4s. 6d.—Steel and Iron, by W. H. Greenwood, F.C.S., Assoc. M.I.C.E., &c., 5s.—Spinning Woollen and Worsted, by W. S. Bright McLaren, 4s. 6d.—Design in Textile Fabrics, by T. R. Ashenhurst, 4s. 6d.—Practical Mechanics, by Prof. Perry, M.E., 3s. 6d.—Cutting Tools Worked by Hand and Machine, by Prof. Smith, 3s. 6d.

Other Volumes in preparation. A Prospectus sent post free on application.

Books for Young People,

"Little Folks" Half-Yearly Volume. With 200 Illustrations, 3s. 6d.; or cloth gilt, 5s.

Bo-Peep. A Book for the Little Ones. With Original Stories and Verses, Illustrated throughout. Boards, 2s. 6d.; cloth gilt, 3s. 6d.

The World's Lumber Room. By SELINA GAYE. Illustrated. 3s. 6d.

The "Proverbs" Series. Consisting of a New and Original Series of Stories by Popular Authors, founded on and illustrating well-known Proverbs. With Four Illustrations in each Book, printed on a tint. Crown 8vo, 160 pages, cloth, 1s. 6d. each.

FRITTERS; OR, "IT'S A LONG LANE THAT HAS NO TURNING." By Sarah Pitt.

TRIXY; OR, "THOSE WHO LIVE IN GLASS HOUSES SHOULDN'T THROW STONES." By Maggie Symington.

THE TWO HARDCASTLES; OR, "A FRIEND IN NEED IS A FRIEND INDEED." By Madeline Bonavia Hunt.

MAJOR MONK'S MOTTO; OR, "LOOK BEFORE YOU LEAP." By the Rev. F. Langbridge.

TIM THOMSON'S TRIAL; OR, "ALL IS NOT GOLD THAT GLITTERS." By George Weatherly.

URSULA'S STUMBLING-BLOCK; OR, "PRIDE COMES BEFORE A FALL." By Julia Goddard.

RUTH'S LIFE-WORK; OR, "NO PAINS, NO GAINS." By the Rev. Joseph Johnson.

The "Cross and Crown" Series. Consisting of Stories founded on incidents which occurred during Religious Persecutions of Past Days. With Four Illustrations in each Book, printed on a tint. Crown 8vo, 256 pages, 2s. 6d. each.

BY FIRE AND SWORD: A STORY OF THE HUGUENOTS. By Thomas Archer.

ADAM HEPBURN'S VOW: A TALE OF KIRK AND COVENANT. By Annie S. Swan.

NO. XIII.; OR, THE STORY OF THE LOST VESTAL. A Tale of Early Christian Days. By Emma Marshall.

The World's Workers. A Series of New and Original Volumes. With Portraits printed on a tint as Frontispiece. 1s. each.

CHARLES DICKENS. By his Eldest Daughter.

SIR TITUS SALT AND GEORGE MOORE. By J. Burnley.

FLORENCE NIGHTINGALE, CATHERINE MARSH, FRANCES RIDLEY HAVERGAL, MRS. RANYARD ("L.N.R."). By Lizzie Aldridge.

DR. GUTHRIE, FATHER MATHEW, ELIHU BURRITT, JOSEPH LIVESEY. By the Rev. J. W. Kirton.

SIR HENRY HAVELOCK AND COLIN CAMPBELL, LORD CLYDE. By E. C. Phillips.

ABRAHAM ·LINCOLN. By Ernest Foster.

DAVID LIVINGSTONE. By Robert Smiles.

GEORGE MÜLLER AND ANDREW REED. By E. R. Pitman.

RICHARD COBDEN. By R. Gowing.

BENJAMIN FRANKLIN. By E. M. Tomkinson.

HANDEL. By Eliza Clarke.

TURNER, THE ARTIST. By the Rev. S. A. Swaine.

GEORGE AND ROBERT STEPHENSON. By C. L. Matéaux.

The "Chimes" Series. Each containing 64 pages, with Illustrations on every page, and handsomely bound in cloth, 1s.

BIBLE CHIMES. Contains Bible Verses for Every Day in the Month.

DAILY CHIMES. Verses from the Poets for Every Day in the Month.

HOLY CHIMES. Verses for Every Sunday in the Year.

OLD WORLD CHIMES. Verses from old writers for Every Day in the Month.

New Books for Boys. With Original Illustrations, produced in a tint. Cloth gilt, 5s. each.

"FOLLOW MY LEADER;" OR, THE BOYS OF TEMPLETON. By Talbot Baines Reed.

FOR FORTUNE AND GLORY: A STORY OF THE SOUDAN WAR. By Lewis Hough.

THE CHAMPION OF ODIN; OR, VIKING LIFE IN THE DAYS OF OLD. By J. Fred. Hodgetts.

BOUND BY A SPELL; OR THE HUNTED WITCH OF THE FOREST. By the Hon. Mrs. Greene.

Price 3s. 6d. each.

ON BOARD THE "ESMERALDA;" OR, MARTIN LEIGH'S LOG. By John C. Hutcheson.

IN QUEST OF GOLD; OR, UNDER THE WHANGA FALLS. By Alfred St. Johnston.

FOR QUEEN AND KING; OR, THE LOYAL 'PRENTICE. By Henry Frith.

The "Boy Pioneer" Series. By EDWARD S. ELLIS. With Four Full-page Illustrations in each Book. Crown 8vo, cloth, 2s. 6d. each.

NED IN THE WOODS. A Tale of Early Days in the West.

NED ON THE RIVER. A Tale of Indian River Warfare.

NED IN THE BLOCK HOUSE. A Story of Pioneer Life in Kentucky.

The "Log Cabin" Series. By EDWARD S. ELLIS. With Four Full-page Illustrations in each. Crown 8vo, cloth, 2s. 6d. each.

THE LOST TRAIL. | CAMP-FIRE AND WIGWAM.

Sixpenny Story Books. All Illustrated, and containing Interesting Stories by well-known Writers.

LITTLE CONTENT.
THE SMUGGLER'S CAVE.
LITTLE LIZZIE.
LITTLE BIRD.
THE BOOT ON THE WRONG FOOT.
LUKE BARNICOTT.
LITTLE PICKLES.
THE BOAT CLUB. By Oliver Optic.

HELPFUL NELLIE; AND OTHER STORIES.
THE ELCHESTER COLLEGE BOYS.
MY FIRST CRUISE.
LOTTIE'S WHITE FROCK.
ONLY JUST ONCE.
THE LITTLE PEACEMAKER.
THE DELFT JUG. By Silverpen.

The "Baby's Album" Series. Four Books, each containing about 50 Illustrations. Price 6d. each; or cloth gilt, 1s. each.

BABY'S ALBUM.
DOLLY'S ALBUM.

FAIRY'S ALBUM.
PUSSY'S ALBUM.

Illustrated Books for the Little Ones. Containing interesting Stories. All Illustrated. 1s. each.

INDOORS AND OUT.
SOME FARM FRIENDS.
THOSE GOLDEN SANDS.
LITTLE MOTHERS AND THEIR CHILDREN.

OUR PRETTY PETS.
OUR SCHOOLDAY HOURS.
CREATURES TAME.
CREATURES WILD.

Shilling Story Books. All Illustrated, and containing Interesting Stories.

THORNS AND TANGLES.
THE CUCKOO IN THE ROBIN'S NEST.
JOHN'S MISTAKE.
PEARL'S FAIRY FLOWER.
THE HISTORY OF FIVE LITTLE PITCHERS.
DIAMONDS IN THE SAND.
SURLY BOB.
THE GIANT'S CRADLE.

SHAG AND DOLL.
AUNT LUCIA'S LOCKET.
THE MAGIC MIRROR.
THE COST OF REVENGE.
CLEVER FRANK.
AMONG THE REDSKINS.
THE FERRYMAN OF BRILL.
HARRY MAXWELL.
A BANISHED MONARCH.

"Little Folks" Painting Books. With Text, and Outline Illustrations for Water-Colour Painting. **1s.** each.

FRUITS AND BLOSSOMS FOR "LITTLE FOLKS" TO PAINT.
THE "LITTLE FOLKS" PROVERB PAINTING BOOK.
THE "LITTLE FOLKS" ILLUMINATING BOOK.

PICTURES TO PAINT.
"LITTLE FOLKS" PAINTING BOOK.
"LITTLE FOLKS" NATURE PAINTING BOOK.
ANOTHER "LITTLE FOLKS" PAINTING BOOK.

Eighteenpenny Story Books. All Illustrated throughout.

THREE WEE ULSTER LASSIES.
LITTLE QUEEN MAB.
UP THE LADDER.
DICK'S HERO: AND OTHER STORIES.
THE CHIP BOY.
RAGGLES, BAGGLES, and the EMPEROR.
ROSES FROM THORNS.
FAITH'S FATHER.

BY LAND AND SEA.
THE YOUNG BERRINGTONS.
JEFF AND LEFF.
TOM MORRIS'S ERROR.
WORTH MORE THAN GOLD.
"THROUGH FLOOD — THROUGH FIRE;" AND OTHER STORIES.
THE GIRL WITH THE GOLDEN LOCKS.
STORIES OF THE OLDEN TIME.

The "Cosy Corner" Series. Story Books for Children. Each containing nearly ONE HUNDRED PICTURES. **1s. 6d.** each.

SEE-SAW STORIES.
LITTLE CHIMES FOR ALL TIMES.
WEE WILLIE WINKIE.
PET'S POSY OF PICTURES AND STORIES.
DOT'S STORY BOOK.
STORY FLOWERS for RAINY HOURS.

LITTLE TALKS with LITTLE PEOPLE
BRIGHT RAYS FOR DULL DAYS.
CHATS FOR SMALL CHATTERERS.
PICTURES FOR HAPPY HOURS.
UPS AND DOWNS OF A DONKEY'S LIFE.

The "World in Pictures." Illustrated throughout. **2s. 6d.** each.

A RAMBLE ROUND FRANCE.
ALL THE RUSSIAS.
CHATS ABOUT GERMANY.
THE LAND OF THE PYRAMIDS (EGYPT).
PEEPS INTO CHINA.

THE EASTERN WONDERLAND (JAPAN).
GLIMPSES OF SOUTH AMERICA.
ROUND AFRICA.
THE LAND OF TEMPLES (INDIA).
THE ISLES OF THE PACIFIC.

Two-Shilling Story Books. All Illustrated.

STORIES OF THE TOWER.
MR. BURKE'S NIECES.
MAY CUNNINGHAM'S TRIAL.
THE TOP OF THE LADDER: How TO REACH IT.
LITTLE FLOTSAM.
MADGE AND HER FRIENDS.
THE CHILDREN OF THE COURT.
A MOONBEAM TANGLE.
MAID MARJORY.

THE FOUR CATS OF THE TIPPERTONS.
MARION'S TWO HOMES.
LITTLE FOLKS' SUNDAY BOOK.
TWO FOURPENNY BITS.
POOR NELLY.
TOM HERIOT.
THROUGH PERIL TO FORTUNE.
AUNT TABITHA'S WAIFS.
IN MISCHIEF AGAIN.

Half-Crown Story Books.

MARGARET'S ENEMY.
PEN'S PERPLEXITIES.
NOTABLE SHIPWRECKS.
GOLDEN DAYS.
WONDERS OF COMMON THINGS.
LITTLE EMPRESS JOAN.
TRUTH WILL OUT.

SOLDIER AND PATRIOT (George Washington).
PICTURES OF SCHOOL LIFE AND BOYHOOD.
THE YOUNG MAN IN THE BATTLE OF LIFE. By the Rev Dr. Landels.
THE TRUE GLORY OF WOMAN By the Rev. Dr. Landels.

Library of Wonders. Illustrated Gift-books for Boys. **2s. 6d. each.**

WONDERFUL ADVENTURES.
WONDERS OF ANIMAL INSTINCT.
WONDERS OF ARCHITECTURE.
WONDERS OF ACOUSTICS.

WONDERS OF WATER.
WONDERFUL ESCAPES.
BODILY STRENGTH AND SKILL.
WONDERFUL BALLOON ASCENTS.

Gift Books for Children. With Coloured Illustrations. **2s. 6d. each.**

THE STORY OF ROBIN HOOD.
SANDFORD AND MERTON.

TRUE ROBINSON CRUSOES.
REYNARD THE FOX.

THE PILGRIM'S PROGRESS.

Three and Sixpenny Library of Standard Tales, &c. All Illustrated and bound in cloth gilt. Crown 8vo. **3s. 6d. each.**

JANE AUSTEN AND HER WORKS.
BETTER THAN GOOD.
MISSION LIFE IN GREECE AND PALESTINE.
THE DINGY HOUSE AT KENSINGTON.
THE ROMANCE OF TRADE.
THE THREE HOMES.
MY GUARDIAN.
SCHOOL GIRLS.

DEEPDALE VICARAGE.
IN DUTY BOUND.
THE HALF SISTERS.
PEGGY OGLIVIE'S INHERITANCE.
THE FAMILY HONOUR.
ESTHER WEST.
WORKING TO WIN.
KRILOF AND HIS FABLES. By W. R. S. Ralston, M.A.
FAIRY TALES. By Prof. Morley.

The Home Chat Series. All Illustrated throughout. Fcap. 4to. Boards, **3s. 6d. each.** Cloth, gilt edges, **5s. each.**

HALF-HOURS WITH EARLY EXPLORERS.
STORIES ABOUT ANIMALS.
STORIES ABOUT BIRDS.
PAWS AND CLAWS.
HOME CHAT.

SUNDAY CHATS WITH OUR YOUNG FOLKS.
PEEPS ABROAD FOR FOLKS AT HOME.
AROUND AND ABOUT OLD ENGLAND.

Books for the Little Ones.

THE LITTLE DOINGS OF SOME LITTLE FOLKS. By Chatty Cheerful. Illustrated. **5s.**
THE SUNDAY SCRAP BOOK. With One Thousand Scripture Pictures. Boards, **5s.**; cloth, **7s. 6d.**
DAISY DIMPLE'S SCRAP BOOK. Containing about 1,000 Pictures. Boards, **5s.**; cloth gilt, **7s. 6d.**
LESLIE'S SONGS FOR LITTLE FOLKS. Illustrated. **1s. 6d.**

LITTLE FOLKS' PICTURE ALBUM With 168 Large Pictures. **5s.**
LITTLE FOLKS' PICTURE GALLERY. With 150 Illustrations. **5s.**
THE OLD FAIRY TALES. With Original Illustrations. Boards, **1s.**; cloth, **1s. 6d.**
MY DIARY. With 12 Coloured Plates and 366 Woodcuts. **1s.**
THREE WISE OLD COUPLES. With 16 Coloured Plates. **5s.**

Books for Boys.

KING SOLOMON'S MINES. By H. Rider Haggard. **5s.**
THE SEA FATHERS. By Clements Markham. Illustrated. **2s. 6d.**
TREASURE ISLAND. By R. L. Stevenson. With Full-page Illustrations. **5s.**
HALF-HOURS WITH EARLY EXPLORERS. By T. Frost. Illustrated. Cloth gilt, **5s.**

MODERN EXPLORERS. By Thomas Frost. Illustrated. **5s.**
CRUISE IN CHINESE WATERS. By Capt. Lindley. Illustrated. **5s.**
WILD ADVENTURES IN WILD PLACES. By Dr. Gordon Stables, M.D., R.N. Illustrated. **5s.**
JUNGLE, PEAK, AND PLAIN. By Dr. Gordon Stables, R.N. Illustrated. **5s.**

CASSELL & COMPANY, Limited, London, Paris, New York and Melbourne.

www.ingramcontent.com/pod-product-compliance
Lightning Source LLC
Chambersburg PA
CBHW030618270326
41927CB00007B/1217